To Tame a Savage Heart

To Tame a
Savage
Heart

*The first Wycliffe missionary translators to
the Secoya and Orejon Indian tribes of the Amazon
jungle in Peru, South America*

Robert H. Sandberg

Essence
PUBLISHING

Belleville, Ontario, Canada

To Tame a Savage Heart
Copyright © 1999, Robert H. Sandberg

Unless otherwise indicated, all Scripture quotations are taken from the *New American Standard Bible* (Copyright © 1960, 1962, 1963, 1968, 1971, 1972, 1973, 1975, 1977 by The Lockman Foundation. Used by permission.)

Scriptures marked *JB* are taken from *The Jerusalem Bible* (Copyright © 1966, 1967, 1968 by Darton, Longman & Todd Ltd. and Doubleday & Company Inc.)

Scriptures marked *TEV* are taken from the *Good News Bible—The Bible in Today's English Version* (Copyright © 1976 by The American Bible Society.)

ISBN: 1-894169-70-0

Essence Publishing is a Christian Book Publisher dedicated to furthering the work of Christ through the written word. For more information, contact: 44 Moira Street West, Belleville, Ontario, Canada K8P 1S3. Phone: 1-800-238-6376. Fax: (613) 962-3055.
E-mail: info@essence.on.ca
Internet: www.essence.on.ca

Printed in Canada
by

Essence
PUBLISHING

Dedication

"Wherever you go, I will go; wherever you live, I will live. Your people will be my people, and your God will be my God...." These were the words Ruth, of the Old Testament, said to Naomi (Ruth 1:16, TEV).

My wife, Ruth, maintained the same attitude Ruth of the Old Testament had. Ruth made a home for us no matter how primitive or difficult the circumstances. She has continued to be my help-mate for more than fifty years, and has helped in reconstructing many of the events of this story. She also spent many hours entering the manuscript into the computer.

Table of Contents

Acknowledgements

I WISH TO THANK THE PERUVIAN ARMY AND POLICE Department for their work in freeing the Orejones from slavery. Without their valued help, it would not have happened.

I also want to thank my daughter Barbara for her suggestions and input as I wrote, and rewrote, and rewrote this story.

I especially want to thank Elaine Colvin of Writer's Information Network for her invaluable input into this project. Without her encouragement and help, I'm not sure I would have stuck with it. Writing is hard work.

Preface

"DAY BY DAY THE LORD ADDED TO THEIR (CHRIS-tian) community those destined to be saved." We read these words in the Book of Acts, the end of chapter two where Peter had been preaching Christ to the crowds at Jerusalem. The Book of Acts is full of "success" stories as the apostles went about preaching the Good News.

"The word of the Lord continued to spread: the number of disciples in Jerusalem was greatly increased and a large group of priests made their submission to the faith" (Acts 6:7, JB).

When we feel the call into the Lord's work (as well as into secular work), we all look forward to being successful as man equates success. In the eyes of man, some would be labeled as failures because large numbers of believers were not added to the church. Some workers struggle for years without seeing any visible signs of fruit.

I am reminded of what my pastor said to me as I poured out my heart to him. I was discouraged. "Just remember this, Bob, maybe God has called you to be a planter. Someone else may be called to do the watering, but ultimately, it is God who gives the increase. Don't ever lose sight of that." I needed that encouragement from Pastor Peterson.

As you will read in the following pages, our ministry was not punctuated with great successes as man views success, but it is comforting to know that God rewards the obedience of His children.

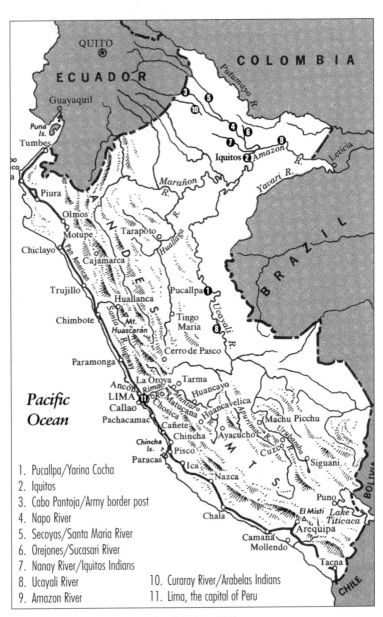

1. Pucallpa/Yarina Cocha
2. Iquitos
3. Cabo Pantoja/Army border post
4. Napo River
5. Secoyas/Santa Maria River
6. Orejones/Sucasari River
7. Nanay River/Iquitos Indians
8. Ucayali River
9. Amazon River
10. Curaray River/Arabelas Indians
11. Lima, the capital of Peru

PERU

1 | Culture Shock

THE CACKLE OF CHICKENS, THE GRUNTS OF PIGS, and the engine noise broke the stillness of the Peruvian jungle as the jeep jostled along the dusty, bumpy road that led to Yarina Cocha. Smoke curled upward from the open fires in front of the few native huts scattered here and there along the shore of Palm Lake, the English name for Yarina Cocha. The mission compound, built along the shore of this beautiful black-water lake nestled among tall tropical trees, would become our base camp and lifeline to civilization for the next five years.

The year was 1953, the year Dwight David Eisenhower was inaugurated as the thirty-fourth president of the United States. Ruth and I had graduated from college, completed the required missionary training, and were eager to serve God, to turn the world up-side-down for Christ.

It seemed like a dream that we were finally here after years of preparation. Only a few days before, we had boarded the DC-3 plane at the Houston, Texas airport, and were

13

on our way with a stop-over in Panama. The temperature in Panama was above 100°F, and inside the tiny airport waiting room it was even hotter, so we stood outside watching the men transfer luggage to another airplane.

While standing next to the wire fence, we noticed a luggage tag being blown down the runway, then it veered in our direction and landed at our feet. I picked it up. It was a tag from our luggage. Had it not come our way, and had I not picked it up, who knows where our luggage would have gone? We gave the ticket to one of the men handling the luggage. He mumbled something in Spanish, located our luggage, and reattached the missing tag. After about an hour of sweating in the hot sun, we were again aboard another DC-3 and heading for Lima, Peru, South America.

We were met at the Lima airport by the Wycliffe group home housemother, Mrs. Cudney. She was a dear lady whose life was dedicated to helping others.

The Cudneys had owned and operated a wholesale meat company in Chicago. They were upper middle-class people whose lives were filled with young people. As she put it, "Our home was like Grand Central Station."

Mr. Cudney had passed away suddenly from a heart attack at the height of his career. They owned a lovely home and were financially secure, but it all came to a sudden and tragic end when he died in his fifties.

Their son and two foster daughters were grown and away from home. One of the foster daughters and her husband were members of Wycliffe Bible Translators. One day Harriet, seeing the loneliness in her mother's life, suggested, "Wycliffe is in need of a housemother at the group home in Lima. Would you consider filling that need?"

Grandma Cudney (as she was affectionately called) responded immediately. That was just what she needed—to be needed. She sold the family home, packed up, and came to another Grand Central Station.

As soon as we cleared customs in Lima, we were met with the usual warm smile of Grandma Cudney and her bouquet of flowers. We were then whisked off through the narrow, over-crowded streets of Lima to the group home. My first impression of Lima was the traffic. They drove by the horn (later outlawed). "He who honks first has right-of-way," Mrs. Cudney explained as our driver honked his way through the maze of snarled traffic. It seemed as though every driver loved to play the game of "chicken."

Lima House was a home away from home and Grandma Cudney made everyone feel very special. When we had to go to Lima for dental work or medical problems the base doctor was not equipped to handle, to purchase needed items not available in the jungle, or just plain R & R, we could always count on a good bed and wonderful meals.

Like all big cities, Lima, Peru, is a busy place with its usual traffic jams. Only Lima is worse. The downtown streets are very narrow. More cars seem to be added without widening the streets.

Besides buses, Lima has a unique public transportation system. Taxies can either be taxies or *colectivos*. If taxi business is slow, they become *colectivos* and follow the same route as the buses picking up passengers. They charge a little more, but they're usually more comfortable than the over-crowded buses.

Mrs. Cudney related the following story. "I was riding downtown in a *colectivo* last week. Every time we came to an intersection, the driver crossed himself. I thought, *My, this fellow is certainly religious.* When we finally arrived downtown, the driver let out a sigh of relief.

"Why did you let out a sigh?" I asked.

"I don't have any brakes," the man answered.

Lima House, as the group home is called, was built much like American motels without the yellow lines for parking cars. Each motel unit has a private bath and is large enough to accommodate a family. One wing contains the dining room and a *sala* (living room).

After a few days' rest from the long flight from America, we were in the air again across the breath-taking Andes Mountains. We looked down at an "artist's painting" of phosphorescent blue lakes that looked like blue diamonds set in a patchwork of white snow, and jutting, jagged rocky peaks. And then the carpet of lush green jungle loomed ahead of us, stretching as far as the eye could see. Here and there colorful birds skimmed across the tree tops looking for jungle fruits to feast on.

As we stepped out of the plane at the airport outside the little jungle town of Pucallpa, the stifling, oppressive jungle heat engulfed us. Perspiration poured down our faces. Our clothing clung to us. It was hot and humid. The jungle, we learned, has four climates: hot and hotter, wet and wetter.

The Yarina Cocha compound is made up of houses scattered here and there. Some of the houses overlook the lake; others were built wherever there was a space big enough for a house. A few were built with thatched roofs, but the majority have aluminum or galvanized, corrugated roofing from which rain water used to be collected in barrels and piped into the houses. The resident medical doctor later tested the lake water for bacteria and discovered the water was safe to use in the homes. No more need for rain barrels.

Unlike the native huts, the *Gringo* houses have wooden floors and screened-in walls for privacy (and to keep out the squadrons of insects that inhabit the jungle), with the usual American kitchen, bathroom, living room, and bedrooms. The missionaries try to live as comfortably as possible in a hostile environment.

In contrast, most of the native houses don't have walls. They have split palm bark floors, and are built 2 to 3 feet off the ground to keep out the animals. Chickens and pigs roam freely about picking up bits and pieces of the discarded family meal of plantains, fish, and cassava roots.

The Yarina Cocha compound is equipped with an airplane hangar and repair shop, offices, a radio shack and tower, commissary, telephones, plus a generator to supply the electricity. A school for the children of the missionaries is also located here.

Yarina Cocha is the hub of Wycliffe Bible Translators in Peru. From here linguists work with the more than forty language groups. They spend several weeks or months in the tribal villages and then return to the base to analyze and learn the language. Periodically, they bring Indian informants from the tribe to the base for concentrated study, free from the everyday interruptions and demands placed upon missionary linguists: treating the common cold, eye infections, injuries, and a host of other maladies. Near the base are houses for select Indians who are brought to the base each year to attend a teacher training course. Upon graduation, the Indians return to their respective villages as teachers. The course also trains Indian medical technicians to treat the tribes' many illnesses, thus relieving the translator to work on the language.

One evening, as Ruth and I were strolling around the

base, we met our director, Cameron Townsend (known as Uncle Cam). After the usual "Good evening," Uncle Cam asked, "Would you and Ruth consider going to the Secoya Tribe? They are located near the Peruvian/Ecuadorian border up the Napo River. I am suggesting you because you don't have children. The Secoyas would be a difficult situation for a family. Pray about it and let me know."

Wycliffe is a rather loosely knit organization. Each member is generally allowed to move "as the Lord leads." However, when Uncle Cam suggested something, there was an air of more than just a suggestion. It became a compelling request.

A few days later we were invited to have dinner with Uncle Cam and his wife, Elaine.

"Have you considered the Secoyas?" he asked.

"Yes, we have. We would like to work among the Secoyas."

"Good, I was hoping you would. A few years ago I was at the Army post at Cabo Pantoja on the Peruvian border and saw two of the colorful Secoya men. They live much as they did thousands of years ago. My heart went out to them. They, too, need the Bible translated into their language."

"How soon should we plan to go?" was our first question.

"I would like you to go as soon as possible. First, though, Bob will have to make a survey trip to locate the tribe because they live hidden in the jungle. Gene Minor would be the perfect person to go with you."

Gene and Dorothy were working among the Huitoto Indians some distance below the mouth of the Napo River, on one of the small tributaries of the Amazon River.

They would live with the Huitotos for several months gathering linguistic data, then return to Yarina Cocha to process those materials. Often they would bring one or more of the Indians to the base for more concentrated study.

Gene and Dorothy had just recently arrived back at the base, so Gene was free to accompany me. Rather, I would accompany him because he spoke Spanish and would be my first teacher of the mysteries of the jungle and its inhabitants.

Our next project: locate the Secoyas and obtain their permission to live among them.

2 | The Land of the Secoyas

THE JUNGLE OF PERU IS UNLIKE THE JUNGLE OF southern Mexico where we had gone for jungle training to prepare us for life in the tropics. Southern Mexico is made up of mountains. The Peruvian Jungle is not. It is a vast area of an unending sea of green as far as the eye can see, and beyond.

To the west are the Andes Mountains—the Cordillera Huascaran rises to a height of 22,205 feet. To the east stretches the verdant green, yellow, and red painted jungle, broken only by the snaking Amazon River as it winds its way through Peru and Brazil, finally reaching the Atlantic Ocean.

Not realizing the difference between the Mexican Jungle and the Peruvian Jungle, I found myself without adequate footwear. In Mexico I could wear leather work shoes, but because of the swamps in the Amazon, I could not. In all our buying for life in Peru, we overlooked one important item—adequate shoes. We hadn't purchased tennis shoes. I guess we weren't planning on playing tennis.

Gene and I packed what bare essentials we would need from the base: jungle hammocks, sleeping bags, cooking utensils, and clothing. Food and trade goods we could purchase in Iquitos, the large town on the upper Amazon River where the float plane would stop to refuel.

We stuffed what we figured to be our essential equipment into the tiny Cessna 180 float plane, and after a round of prayers with our wives and friends, we were soon bouncing along the lake and airborne, bound for Iquitos.

Iquitos is the inland trade center for the upper Amazon. Large ships from many parts of the world come here to bring consumer goods and pick up raw materials from the jungle: peccary (wild pig) skins, jungle rubber, rose wood oil, lumber, and other items used in the manufacture of goods sold to the world.

Iquitos has one dirt-road main street that turns into mud each time the tropical rains hit—which is often. Vendors ply the streets, pushing their two-wheeled carts, hawking locally made charcoal for cooking. (Dry wood is split and stacked into piles then covered with dirt leaving a small hole for lighting. As the wood smolders it does not burn completely. The blackened coal-like wood is then sold for cooking).

Other two-wheeled venders sell milk—whole milk costs the most, milk mixed with one-third water costs less, and milk mixed with one-half water is the least expensive. I never did understand why the consumer couldn't mix his own water with the milk if they wanted thinner milk.

Bunches of freshly-made spaghetti hang overhead in front of the bakeries, drying from the wind and hot sun, ready to be sold.

The loud sound of an auctioneer's rapid-fire chatter can be heard for blocks as he auctions off bolts of cloth recently delivered by ship from England.

The flight from Yarina Cocha to Iquitos is about four and a half hours by Cessna 180 (see map). As rapidly as possible, we purchased the supplies we guessed we would need: colorful beads, spoons, mirrors, knives, machetes, and other trinkets for trading purposes. My feet are longer than the Peruvians'. The largest size shoes I could find in Iquitos were still tight on my feet, but I didn't have any other choice, so I purchased a pair, hoping I could wear them.

The pilot was waiting for us at the plane, ready to go. We loaded our purchases into the plane and were soon airborne for Cabo Pantoja, the army post on the bank of the Napo River just across from Ecuador.

Our pilot radioed ahead so the army post would know we were coming. The commander, *Commandant* Barbis, personally met us at the river's edge. He didn't speak English and I, at this point, didn't speak much Spanish, so Gene had to do all the talking.

The Commander was a very warm and friendly person, but one who portrayed the demeanor of a seasoned officer. "The two of you will stay with me and my wife," he ordered.

Were we honored guests, or was he just keeping a close watch on us? He was probably wondering why two *Gringos* would want to leave the comforts of home to live in such a desolate place, and with savage Indians, as he called them.

After getting situated in the commander's home, he took us to the officers' dining hall. The first course was a bowl of soup. Dinner was always served after 8:00 p.m., and since Gene and I hadn't eaten since breakfast, we were hungry. We devoured all of our soup. However, we noted the others only ate about half and left the rest.

The next course was a salad. Gene and I devoured the salad, but we again noticed the others only ate a portion and left the rest.

The third course was a meat dish. Again, Gene and I ate all ours. The others didn't. We didn't know their custom was to serve six-course meals, but not to eat all of each. By the time we had finished the fourth course, we were stuffed. We had just learned a very valuable lesson in Peruvian eating habits.

We needed a guide to take us to the Secoya Indians. "*Commandant*, do you know anyone who could guide us to the Secoyas?" Gene asked.

"Yes, there is a man whose mother is Secoya. Juan lives at Mira Flores, about thirty minutes by outboard motor down the Napo River."

The commander was again a most gracious host and ordered a subordinate to take us to Mira Flores in one of the base canoes. As we stepped out of the canoe, a man came walking toward us.

Gene held out his hand and with the usual greeting of "*Buenos diaz*," said he was looking for a man named Juan.

"I am Juan," he answered. "What can I do for you?"

"We would like to go to the Secoyas to get permission for my friend and his wife to live among them and learn their language. Would you be willing to take us?"

"Of course," he replied without hesitating. "How much will you pay me?"

"How much do you want?" Gene asked.

"For five *soles* (the Peruvian legal tender) a day I will take you."

"Can you round up two other men? *Don* Roberto and I

will have several bags to take with us. We will pay them the same."

"Yes, I know two men who will go with us. How soon do you want to go?" Juan asked.

"Could we leave day after tomorrow?"

"We will be ready," Juan assured us.

Juan was the perfect choice because his mother was Secoya and he knew enough of the Secoya language to be able to communicate with the Indians and be able to explain why we wanted to live among them.

Juan also hired a third carrier to carry our personal needs for the trip—all the comforts we *Gringos* need to survive, especially our mosquito-proof jungle hammocks.

Early the second morning we set out by trail through the jungle. I was to learn something new about the jungle. I had always been led to believe a jungle is an impregnable mass of tangled brush. The virgin jungle we entered was like walking through a park. The huge trees, each striving to reach higher than the rest to gain access to the sun and open sky, formed a thick canopy of leaves and branches. The sun was above them somewhere, but we couldn't see it.

Only when the jungle is cut and the sun allowed to penetrate do the dormant seeds germinate and the thick brush begins to grow.

Each carrier made a head-strap from the inner bark of a tree. From jungle vines they wove baskets into which they divided our blankets, hammocks, food, medicines, and trade goods. The head-straps, fastened to the baskets, left their hands free to carry their machetes and muzzle loaders. Modern shotguns aren't practical in the hot, humid, jungle because the humidity causes the shells to swell until they won't enter the chamber.

We'd walked about an hour when we came to our first swamp—a large body of water encircling trees that are armor-protected by porcupine-like needles. (The swamps are just an extension of an over-flowing river after a heavy tropical downpour.)

We hadn't been in the swamp long when Gene said, "Are the same thoughts going through your mind that are going through mine?"

"You mean, what's living in this swamp? Like caiman (South American alligator), boa constrictors, sting rays, and more?" I answered.

"That's exactly what I have been thinking," he said.

The cloth tennis shoes I had purchased in Iquitos must have shrunk, or my feet swelled, because they were killing me. Besides, they were sopping wet as was the rest of me.

I finally took off my shoes, took out my knife and cut a hole in the end for my toes. That helped some.

We waded in water up to our necks for about three hours until we finally emerged.

Night falls rapidly in the jungle. By 5:00 p.m. we had to start looking for a place to camp. Just before we were ready to stop for the night, Juan stopped quickly, listened, then slowly walked to his right. He raised his muzzle loader and—"bang." He walked a short distance and picked up our supper—a very large bird. His sight and hearing were uncanny.

Gene had purchased a quantity of rice, so with the rice and bird, we had a very fine feast.

We looked for two sturdy trees from which to sling our hammocks, unpacked our jungle hammocks and some dry clothing, crawled in, and were soon fast asleep. We were tired and sleep came quickly.

Juan and the carriers cut palm fronds and made themselves a lean-to to keep out the night rains. Their skin must have been tough, because the mosquitoes didn't seem to bother them.

Except for the swamps, walking through the virgin jungle was like walking on a padded carpet—which is what it was. The collection of years of leaves falling on the ground formed a thick carpet, making walking easy. We did, however, have to cross several streams too large for us to ford. Our carriers felled trees to form a bridge for us to walk across.

"I'm glad to have the trees to walk on. The current is too strong for swimming," I commented to Gene.

"Guess what? I don't know how to swim," Gene informed me.

This really worried me. It must have rained recently because the streams were raging torrents, their banks filled to overflowing. If I had fallen in, I could at least have kept myself afloat and probably made it to the bank somewhere downstream. If Gene had fallen in, he probably would have drowned. Some of the poles the men fell across the streams were pretty small—with nothing to hang on to.

Our guides could see we were not used to jungle life, so for the last couple of streams, by using small poles tied with vines, they made make-shift rails for us. This was a great help and safety device.

Late the next afternoon, as we approached the edge of the village, Juan asked us to stay hidden while he went into the village to get permission for us to come in.

As soon as he told the village men we were there, all the women, children, and most of the men ran into the jungle leaving only three men to greet us. After Juan talked with the three remaining men, he motioned for us to come in.

The three colorful men, dressed in their usual *cushmas*, waited for us. We held out our hand and they took it, our natural *Gringo* method of greeting. They accepted our outstretched hands, even though they may not have understood it. We had a tendency to do a lot of things "our" way.

Not until they had looked us over thoroughly, to see we did not come to harm them, did the women and children and the other men slowly filter back.

The *cushmas* covered the men from their shoulders to their ankles. The women, however, wore only skirts. Their upper bodies were covered with intricately painted designs.

The Secoyas are a short, stocky, muscular people, with shoulder-length, jet black hair. Except for the hair on their heads, they are hairless—no body hair at all. They would have eyebrows, except they pulled them out—rather, their wives were the husband's eyebrow pluckers, and the husbands plucked the wives' brows. For some reason they don't like eyebrows.

After an hour or so, they began to warm up to us. The first thing they wanted to do was paint my face like theirs. I was too tall for them to reach me while I was standing, so I had to sit down. From a red lipstick-like ball, a couple of young men scraped a slender bamboo stick across the dye to pick up the red color and proceeded to run the stick across my face in various directions to form the designs they wanted. When they were through, they stood back to admire their "art." I am not sure what their laughs suggested. I certainly did look different.

As all peoples, they were curious about us—our size, our beards, and our clothing. They would have me hold out my arms so they could stand underneath. They didn't even reach to my extended arms which made them laugh. They laughed easily—at least in our presence.

Their houses are about 80 feet long and 40 feet wide. The grass roof extends to the ground with a small opening cut in one end for entry. The inside is divided into small sections, an area for each of the family group, with hammocks strung between supporting poles for sleeping and small fires smoldering by the side. It took a few minutes for our eyes to get used to the smoky darkness inside.

We were invited to eat with them—boiled wild pig, cassava root, and a piece of flat tortilla-like bread to dip in our soup. They do not have access to salt, so the food tasted rather flat, but was filling.

Gene and I were given a place between two poles to string our hammocks, but sleeping in a smoke-filled room was not the most restful way to sleep. Especially since they would sleep for short periods of time, then awaken to fan their fire. This was their mosquito repellent.

All members of the same family slept in a very large woven hammock—woven from a palm fiber, spun by hand on the side of their legs. Depending on the size of string they wanted, two or more strands of palm fiber are held in one hand while the other end is held taut between their toes. The fibers are then twisted by rubbing the fibers with their hand against their leg.

The next morning, Juan asked the chief if Ruth and I could come to live with them to learn their language. Several of the chief men of the tribe got their heads together and agreed we could come. Juan also asked if they would build a house for us. It would have been very difficult for the two of us to live in a smoke filled, dark hut, with no windows and no ventilation. They said they would.

After a two-day rest, we returned by the same jungle route to Cabo Pantoja where the Cessna 180 was waiting. We thanked *Commandant* Barbis and his wife for their hospitality and flew back to our wives.

Back at Yarina Cocha, Ruth and Dorothy were waiting for us at the dock as the float plane landed on the lake and taxied to shore. They were glad to see us back safe and sound after not hearing from us for more than a week.

Our next step was to prepare for Ruth and me to live and work among the Secoyas.

3 Jungle Trek

KNOWING IT WOULD BE DIFFICULT FOR RUTH TO make the overland trip to the village, we decided to go there via the Santa Maria River, which is navigable after a heavy rain. The trail would then lead us to the village—about a four-hour walk over a very rough path.

We borrowed a 7 h.p. Mercury outboard motor from the base, but we didn't have any idea how much gasoline we would need to get to the village and back because the Santa Maria River had never been surveyed. The river, as shown on the map, was not drawn to scale nor were the curves shown correctly.

To see how far the Mercury would run on a gallon of gasoline, I put in a half gallon and ran it until it quit. Based on that experiment, it would run one hour on a gallon of gasoline. By a wild guess, I decided to take along a 15-gallon drum of outboard gasoline (gasoline mixed with oil).

"Your boxes and barrels from the States just arrived," a voice on the newly installed telephone service informed us.

Now we could begin packing for living among the Secoyas.

We had the boxes and barrels brought to the medical doctor's house, where we were staying, and began the task of repacking what we would need in the Secoya village.

"This is just like Christmas," Ruth commented as we removed item by item the things we had packed a few months before.

Every so often, as we picked up something, we would laugh and comment, "Why did we bring this along?"

"I don't know," the other would reply. It was fun examining the things we had packed back in Seattle.

"Why did I bring along my blowtorch and soldering supplies," I said aloud, not really expecting an answer. We brought a lot of things we would wonder about. When we did our buying for Peru, we didn't have any idea where we would be, so a lot of our buying was purely by guess. Some was based on our experiences from the Mexican jungle camp training—the three months we spent in southern Mexico on a survival training mission before coming to Peru.

"As long as I have them, I might as well take them along with the rest of my tools," I said, not knowing what I would use them for in the middle of a sparsely settled jungle. My tools included socket wrenches, screwdrivers, and assorted mechanic's and carpenter's tools. We would learn later why they were included.

At the base carpenter shop, I made boxes for shipping from cedar boards the termites would leave alone. I made them in the form of cabinets to use in the house the Indians promised to build for us.

When everything we felt we would need for life among the Indians was packed into boxes and barrels, we had them shipped via river boat down the Ucayali River to Iquitos. The river boats don't have regular schedules, so we didn't have any idea when our things would arrive in Iquitos.

Our next project was to pack items we would be needing immediately, and scheduling our trip to Cabo Pantoja, the Army base up the Napo River on the Ecuadorian border. We were required to take along a two-way radio transmitter so we could keep in touch with Yarina Cocha. After getting everything tucked away in the little Aeronca plane, we took off from Yarina Cocha bound for Iquitos where we hoped our cargo would be. We would also purchase staple foods, medicines, and trade goods for bartering with the Indians.

It was a beautiful, tropical, hot, humid day as we taxied out onto the lake. Only a few cumulus clouds dotted the sky like puffs of cotton balls set against the velvet blue. The pilot revved up the engine and we were soon bouncing along the top of the water, and then, up, up, dangling between earth and sky, on our way. We followed the snaking Ucayali River for the next four hours, seeing an occasional barge chugging along, hoping our cargo was already at Iquitos and not on one of those below us. As much as possible, the pilots follow the rivers so they have a place to land should a problem develop with the airplane.

From our previous experience in Mexico, we knew we were not very good at cooking over an open, smoky fire, so at Iquitos we purchased a one-burner kerosene stove and a 5-gallon can of kerosene.

We knew the Indians liked mirrors, ax heads, machetes, soap, and assorted colored beads. We purchased as many of these items as we felt we could carry with us.

Our cargo had not arrived and the shipping company didn't know when it would. Many of the river boats are wood-burning steam engines and have to stop frequently to cut wood to keep them going. They don't make very good time. They also stop frequently to take on more cargo.

At the shipping company office in Iquitos we made arrangements for our cargo to be transshipped up the Napo River to a place called Villa Luisa. Because our cargo had not arrived, we were forced to buy more things in Iquitos. Our plan was to live in the village, and when our cargo arrived at Villa Luisa we would make the trip out to pick it up.

This time we were not as restricted in what we could take because the Beaver, the plane we would be traveling in to Cabo Pantoja, is a lot larger than the Aeronca.

Commandant Barbis and his wife again welcomed us and told us we would be living in their home. They gave us their bedroom. However, we didn't realize their bedroom contained the only double bed in the small house. We wondered why they had to take long naps everyday until we learned they were both trying to sleep on a narrow single bed. His wife was slender, but he wasn't.

"Where can I purchase a large canoe?" I asked the commander. I had explained that we were planning on going up the Santa Maria River to locate the Secoya Indians and we needed a canoe to take us and our supplies there.

Taking charge once again, *Commandant* Barbis came up with a 36-foot hollowed-out canoe—a canoe that was made to be paddled by several men. The price was a bargain. A mere $30 U.S. It was the commander who had told the man how much to charge us.

However, it wasn't made for an outboard motor, so I had to cut the end off and fasten in a transom to hold the motor. By borrowing a hand saw, hammer, and nails, I set about cutting off the end. There were no lumber or hardware stores in Cabo Pantoja; only a very small general store on the bank of the river that sold cloth, a few canned goods, staples, and other odds and ends.

Several smaller canoes were parked on the bank next to the trail that led to the army post. Among them was a canoe that was no longer of service, but it still had some good wood in it. I obtained permission to cut a piece from the side to fashion a transom (the back end of the canoe on which I could attach the outboard motor). For caulking I used what they call *copal*, a tar-like substance that is a by-product of pitch from a certain tree. The tree is wounded at the base and the pitch or sap runs out and forms pools. This pitch is gathered, then set on fire. As the pitch burns, the black *copal* flows out. When it cools it is hard and brittle. The local men taught me how to re-heat the *copal* and mix lard with it to make it pliable.

We needed Juan's services again to help get the 36-foot canoe up the Santa Maria River.

"*Commandant*, do you know where I can locate Juan?" I asked.

"Ask at the store, they can probably tell you," he answered.

"Can you tell me where I can locate Juan?" I asked the young girl behind the counter.

"There are lots of Juans around here. Which Juan are you wanting?" was her reply.

"Three months ago we hired Juan to take us to the Secoyas. His mother is Secoya," I ventured. News travels fast in the jungle so I was sure she was aware of our last trip.

"Oh, that Juan. He is working for Ramon about an hour downriver. His house is the big house on the left," she answered. The place is called Torres Causano."

This gave me a good opportunity to try out the canoe, with the new transom, as well as the motor.

I headed downstream and located his house. There were only two houses between Ramon's and Cabo Pantoja so it wasn't hard to find.

Ramon came out to meet me. "Is Juan here?" I asked. Just then Juan came over to the canoe.

"My wife is here and we need to go up the Santa Maria river to the Secoyas. Will you guide us?" I asked.

"For five *soles* a day I will," he answered. (One dollar was equal to seven *soles* then.)

"Good, how soon can you be ready?" I asked.

"I'm ready now," he answered. He apparently liked the money we paid him before because there aren't many opportunities in that area for earning money. He jumped at the chance to earn a few more *soles*.

Standing under a tree were three husky men, taller than the Secoyas. By their features, I could tell they were from an Indian tribe. Their straight, jet-black hair hung loosely down to their shoulders, partly hiding their round faces. They were built like weight-lifters.

"Who are those men?" I asked Ramon.

"They are Arabela Indians," he answered.

"Do they live around here?" I wanted to know.

"No, their people live over that direction," as he pointed south across the Napo River. "These Arabelas work for me," he said.

I spent the next few minutes compiling a word list from them, but I didn't know when I would be able to get the list back to the base. I tried to talk to them in my limited Spanish, but their Spanish was as limited as mine.

Juan grabbed a few items and stuffed them into a rubberized bag made from muslin, coated with jungle rubber.

The next morning, as we radioed the base, I told of locating three Arabelas. Our director, Cameron Townsend, was glad for the information. Although we knew of the Arabelas, no one knew where they lived. At least we now knew we were in the general area.

"Before we go up the Santa Maria, I would like to hike to the village once more to make sure the village is still there and see if they have built the house they promised," I informed Juan.

"Let's walk in tomorrow," was his quick reply.

We loaded Juan's things into the canoe and returned to Cabo Pantoja.

"Juan and I are going to hike to the village tomorrow," I told Ruth. "We should be back in about six or seven days. I want to make sure they have built us a house so we don't have to live in the darkness and smoke from their fires.

"*Commandant* and Mrs. Barbis have been such wonderful hosts, but I don't want to wear out our welcome. I think it would be better if I stayed at the house where the trail begins, at Mira Flores," Ruth suggested.

Mira Flores consisted of a single house without walls, set back about 300 yards from the Napo. A small stream drifted lazily by—this was their water supply.

The house was about 50 feet by 50 feet, set on tall ironwood posts 8 feet off the ground—high enough to insure the flood waters would not reach them, because the Napo flooded higher at that point. A few pigs and chickens roamed under the house. A Quechua (Inca) man and his wife lived in the house. Why it was called Mira Flores I'll never know—there were no flowers anywhere.

"Juan and I will be gone for several days. You will be fine here," I told Ruth.

This time, however, I didn't take along everything including the kitchen sink. We traveled much lighter. I was learning.

This trip I only needed Juan and one other carrier. Once again the men disappeared into the jungle and soon returned with materials for making packsacks to carry my gear. We started out early in the morning under a clear blue sky. However, a few darkening clouds soon began to form.

"I think we are going to get wet on this trip," Juan warned to himself more than to us.

The jungle became a bit more recognizable this time. The swamp we waded through on the first trip had receded and the ground was reasonably dry. But it did rain, a light warm rain.

That night I rummaged through my gear and pulled out a dry set of clothing, then strung my hammock between two sturdy trees while the two men constructed another *tambito*, a make-shift shelter for the night. The next morning I noticed the two men looking at their feet and laughing.

"What are you laughing at?" I asked.

"A vampire bat bit our feet and sucked out some of our blood," the men responded.

I looked and could barely see tiny pin-pricks on their toes. They must not have lost much blood, because they kept up the same pace as before, carrying my heavy supplies.

Juan again proved invaluable, not only in supplying us with fresh meat along the way, but in communicating with the Indians.

When we entered the village, my heart sank as I looked for the house we were promised.

"They didn't build the house they said they would build," I lamented to Juan.

"I will talk with them again and see if I can get them to build a house for you," Juan agreed.

The Indians seem genuinely glad to see us. Juan, again, asked them to build a house for us. They, again, agreed to do that. Their excuse for why they hadn't built the house was they didn't believe we would return.

I gave out different items I had brought along this time with the promise, through Juan, I would give them more if they would have a house ready when we returned. They all said "*Dea,*" their word for "good."

By now the Indians were getting to know me and were not at all afraid of me—a 6 foot, 1 inch white man. The young boys were especially friendly; the women were more reserved. Several were sick with flu-like symptoms. I gave each a shot of penicillin that night and another in the morning before we left. During the night, one of the women I treated got up and began to flame the fire. I wanted to check her temperature, so I, too, got out of my hammock.

"Roberto," Juan began, "You better get back in your hammock."

"Why?" I inquired. I noticed giggles coming from several areas of the smoke-filled hut.

"They think you got up because you want the lady to go to bed with you." It didn't take me long to get back into my hammock. More giggles.

We rested that day before beginning our journey back to Mira Flores. By now the jungle didn't appear quite so foreboding. In fact, I was rather enjoying the unspoiled beauty—the many beautiful, stately trees, colorful flowers, and sounds, including the mating calls of the many different animals that inhabit the vast jungle.

On the way back, we were rained on several times. Juan kept his gun powder and shot in a waterproof bag tied around his waist. As we were walking, Juan stopped, looked up in a tree and spotted a squirrel. He took careful aim, pulled the trigger—"pop," not a bang. The powder had gotten damp from all the rain. The lead pellets dripped off the end of the gun.

Juan again loaded his black-powder muzzle loader by pouring gunpowder down the barrel, inserting a wad of scraped palm bark and tamping it down with a rod attached to the underside of the gun. Next, he inserted the shot, added more wadding and tapped that down. He then placed a cap under the hammer, aimed again at the squirrel— another "pop."

All this time the squirrel just sat there looking at us, wondering what we were doing. We all laughed at ourselves and the squirrel. Again, Juan loaded his gun. This time it went "bang" and the poor squirrel dropped to the ground. That was our supper.

Two days later we emerged at Mira Flores. The six days had not been a very pleasant experience for Ruth. There was nothing for her to do and no privacy. The Quechua man and his wife spoke a dialect of Quechua. Ruth didn't understand Quechua, and they spoke very little Spanish, so she couldn't even practice her Spanish. She was very relieved and happy to see us.

Before Juan left us to go home, we made plans to travel to the village by way of the winding Santa Maria River. This time, Juan was the only one to go with us and show us the way. After a day's rest at the commander's home, we began packing for the trip up the Santa Maria River.

4 | Uncharted Waters

THE BIG CANOE WAS RATHER HEAVILY LADEN because we were taking enough food for three months, the time we planned to be with the Secoyas on our first trip. We also had a few tools, our trade goods, gasoline, kerosene, and the radio and generator.

Like all the rivers in the Amazon, the Santa Maria is just another winding, twisting "drainage ditch" for the run-off of the torrential tropical rains.

When the natives say a certain place is "five bends" up the river, they only count the half-moon curves; they don't count the squiggly curves. Five bends might be 10 miles.

We weren't making very good time because of the countless trees blown across the river from the storms that hit frequently. Juan had to either chop through the tree trunks, or find a way over, under, or around them.

The Creator of the Universe made wonderful provision for those living in isolated jungles. Long, strong vines, called *tamshi*, hang from trees. The straight grain allows them to be divided and divided and divided until they are as small as a string, which can be woven into thick, strong ropes. The vines are used for tying roof poles, weaving into baskets, and tying up their canoes. We were told these vines are caused from the bite of a large, black ant called *Isula*. The ant is about an inch long, bites from one end and stings from the other. When the ant stings the tree, a vine begins to grow. That's what the Peruvians told us.

There is also a bark from the Setico tree that grows next to the rivers, that when placed in water swells and becomes very slimy. These are placed on a log so a heavy canoe can be slid over the top. Juan used this bark several times on our trip up the Santa Maria River.

Again, Juan's keen hearing and eyesight kept us in fresh meat along the way. Monkey meat tastes much like beef, just a lot tougher. The ones we ate must have been a hundred years old. Anteater meat is tougher yet. The more you chew it, the tougher it seems to get.

We arrived at the trail to the village on the afternoon of the fourth day. Sitting upright in a canoe with no back rest is not my idea of a pleasure trip. And having to start and stop the motor dozens of times a day didn't help, either. But we made it, and getting out of the canoe was a welcome relief.

We decided what items we would need for the night and started walking down the trail. After a brisk four-hour walk, we arrived at the edge of the village.

This time we didn't have to wait at the edge of the village, we just walked right in. The whole village gathered around us. The women were especially interested in Ruth. Was she constructed the same as they? Ruth wore a blouse. They didn't. That seemed to bother them because they wanted to see what she was hiding. They kept poking at her.

To our pleasant surprise, they actually had constructed a small hut for us to live in. They constructed the little house like the Peruvians' houses on the Napo River: the floor about 4 feet off the ground, made from the hard outer bark of a *pona* palm tree. They made crude steps from an old canoe. They are not the most energetic peoples in the world, so their building us a house encouraged us. We really were invited to live among them, and we were happy to have a house of our own and not have to live in a dark, smoky room with the Secoyas.

The village consisted of three long houses. A small clear-water stream gurgled by. The village compound was smaller than a football field with a small plot of cassava root and corn taking up one corner. The ground around the houses was kept free of grass, so when it rained, the area turned to mud.

As we began to unpack, the entire village made themselves at home. Each item we unpacked had to be handled by everyone—and discussed in a language we didn't understand.

We brought along a few magazines with pictures of "our culture." These proved to be very interesting to the people. As we watched them, we noted that it didn't seem to matter if a picture was held right side up (to us) or upside down. They could discuss the picture of a person with his/her feet pointing up as well as down.

Not until we strung our mosquito net and made up our bed did they finally retreat to their houses. However, early the next morning they were back.

They had never seen eating utensils before and what on earth was a fork used for? One of them figured it out—it was for scratching the head.

Ruth had brought along more than one set of knives, forks, and spoons, so she let them handle the ones she put out. But when the food was ready, she would take out a clean set for us to eat with.

We knew we would get some food from them, but we did have our rice, flour, sugar, salt, oatmeal, and canned foods as a supplement.

We learned another lesson in public relations. In our culture one is paid for the amount of work done. We found out that doesn't hold true in all cultures—not among the Secoyas. Although only a few built our house, they all expected the same amount of pay.

Since it was our custom to pay those who worked, we found out who built our house and we paid them in soap, beads, fishhooks, and yardage. It didn't take us long to figure out we had pulled a very serious boo-boo. Immediately we rectified our error and paid them all the same—quite a drain on our supply of trade goods.

We immediately set out to learn their language by choosing an informant—an older gentleman who seemed willing to help us.

We would point to various items and write down what he said, not knowing if he was giving us the name or not.

After a couple weeks of working on the language, we began to pick up a few words and phrases.

I happened to be working with another man one day and was trying to get the negatives—I do and I don't; it is and it isn't.

I came to the word swim and said, "I don't swim." I wrote down phonetically what he said, but when I looked at the phrase, it just didn't fit the pattern. Finally, it dawned on me.

His answer was, "If you don't swim you'll sink." When he

realized I understood, he laughed and laughed—and I joined him.

Food was not very plentiful. Most of the men sat around painting their faces and bodies. The women kept busy spinning *shambira*, weaving hammocks, pounding a bark from a certain tree to form blankets, and sweeping up around the houses. Much of their time, however, was spent in our little house—watching us. That was good for language learning, but not for our privacy.

Only a few of the men seemed to be adept at hunting. What they brought in was not enough to go around. Consequently, we had to depend upon the food we brought along. We could see our three-months' supply was not going to last.

I did take along a shotgun, so one day I decided I would try my luck at hunting. As I walked along a well-worn trail I spotted a monkey high up in the tree. Taking careful aim, I pulled the trigger and the little guy fell to the ground wounded. I really felt terrible. He was screaming at me as if to say, "Why did you shoot me? I didn't do anything to you." I couldn't leave it lying there wounded, so I put it out of its misery. I took it home and we did eat it, but from then on I left the hunting to the Indians.

The lack of privacy was especially hard on Ruth. And not being able to talk in her own language with other English speakers of her gender was causing frustrations that she kept pent up inside.

One night, in the middle of the night, Ruth sat up and said, "It's a sheet!"

"It's a sheet?" I asked.

"It's a box!" she exclaimed.

"It's a box?" I again responded.

"It's a sheet!" she nearly shouted.

"It's a sheet?" I asked.

Then she awoke and said, "Oh, shut up and go back to sleep."

Another night in the early morning, she again sat up quickly and said, "It's an absent going through a moth-eaten hole."

I started to respond when she again woke up and said, "Go back to sleep."

Bathing was another problem for Ruth. The Indian women had a way of getting into the water and removing their skirts without exposing themselves.

To bathe, Ruth wore her bathing suit. This worked fine, except for the spectators lined up along the river bank. They wash their hair every time they get into the river, which was often. Ruth, on the other hand, only washed her hair every other day. If Ruth didn't wash her hair, they would motion for her to put her head under water and wash her hair.

We had been living in the village for three months. Language study was coming along well, but we realized we were going to have to leave because our food was running out. We were also running out of trade goods. We had brought along a 5-gallon metal container of margarine which, in the heat, turned rancid. The Indians were especially fond of soap and it was impossible for them to get it, so we showed them how to make soap using the rancid margarine. For lye, we took ashes from their fires, mixed it with water and slowly let it drip through several layers of cloth. We then added the lye to the margarine and boiled the mixture. It made beautiful white soap that floated. The Indians loved it.

We radioed our base and told them we were coming out. It had rained for several days and we knew the river was high enough for us to travel.

Another thing happened that caused us to realize it was time to leave.

We were sitting in our house. Several Indians were also in the house. Suddenly, one of the ladies came over and, for no apparent reason, slapped Ruth on the side of the face and then walked away. We just sat there stunned.

"Why did she do that?" Ruth asked.

"I have no idea," was my response.

The barter method of handling transactions also wasn't working very well. How do you know how much of what to give someone for doing something? Apparently, we hadn't paid one of the men what he thought he should have received. After paying him, he shook his spear at us. We still didn't know enough of the language to discuss the problem with him.

We never did learn what caused the slapping incident, but we knew we needed to leave. We cranked up the radio and talked with our director, Uncle Cam, to discuss the incident with him. He concurred it was time for us to come out for a rest and re-evaluation of the situation.

At first, the Indians told us they would not carry our things back to the river and canoe, nor accompany us downriver.

Finally, though, three men and a woman agreed to carry our things and paddle the canoe downriver.

The day before we were to leave, a woman died in child birth, but the baby lived. But how were they going to feed the baby? We saw something we didn't know could happen. An older woman, who hadn't had a baby in years, suddenly began nursing the baby and produced milk. If we hadn't seen it we never would have believed it could happen. But it did.

Early the next morning, we took what items we needed and left the rest. All we had for food were two cans of oatmeal—no milk, salt, or sugar.

About an hour downriver, the Indians pulled the canoe to the shore and left. We didn't know where they were going, nor if we were being stranded. However, about an hour later they returned with a large catch of fish. They knew of a lake full of fish and had taken advantage of it.

They shared the fish with us, but other than that, all we ate was oatmeal without salt, sugar, or milk—twice a day. It was years before we could face another bowl of oatmeal. The next day, they spotted a tapir hung up on some brush in the river. They said a jaguar had killed it.

Everyone set about butchering the tapir. As one of the men cut into the stomach, it exploded from the pent-up gasses. He was thoroughly covered with half-digested grass. Of course, everyone laughed as he jumped in the river to wash it off. We camped there that night so they could smoke the meat.

Ruth was so tired she wanted to go to bed without eating anything, but I decided to build a fire and cook more oatmeal. I insisted we both had to eat something, even though it would be more plainly cooked oatmeal. They offered us some of the meat, but we declined. It smelled rotten.

I had a hard time finding enough dry wood to make a fire, but I finally got one going and cooked the oatmeal. It was getting harder and harder to swallow. It had been a long, hard day. We were so tired we crawled into our mosquito nets and were soon asleep. The Indians, however, stayed up all night smoking the tapir.

The next morning, the smoked tapir meat was loaded into our already heavy canoe. As we shoved off, there was only about an inch of freeboard left, which meant there couldn't be much side-to-side movement for fear of filling the canoe with water.

Going was again slow because a recent tropical storm had blown more trees across the river—trees we had to either cut through, go under, over, or around.

One particularly large tree had fallen across the river and was half in the water and half out. It was too large to chop in two, and too large to slide over. We spent at least two hours digging a channel behind the stump. Once we got water to flow in a small stream, we used it to wash a large enough channel for the canoe to pass.

The third day, the Indians again pulled the canoe to the bank and got out.

"We are going to another village. We will be back when the sun is there," the Indian said as he pointed to the sky. We didn't know how long that would be, but we had no choice but to wait and hope they would come back.

We didn't have much oatmeal left, and they took all the smoked tapir meat with them. Had they left some, we probably would have held our noses and eaten enough to satiate our hunger.

We sat there all that day and the next. We were finishing the last of our oatmeal.

"Ruth, I'm going to take my shotgun and walk for two hours into the jungle the direction they went. If I don't find them in two hours, I will return." I hated to leave Ruth by herself while I trudged off into the unfriendly jungle, but there was little choice.

After two hours walking through the jungle, I came to a large swamp, but there was no way through the swamp. The only thing I could do was return to the river where Ruth and the canoe awaited me. *But which way had I come?* I didn't have a compass, and as I looked behind me, all I saw was jungle that all looked the same.

Fear gripped me. *What if I get lost? What would Ruth do?* She couldn't cry for help because no one, other than the Secoyas, lives along the Santa Maria River. She did have the two-way radio, if she could get the generator started. I bowed my head and prayed, "Lord, show me the way," and headed back the way I "thought" I had come.

To the relief of both of us, I came out at the canoe. Ruth was almost in tears. The same thoughts had gone through her mind, *what if?*

"If you hadn't come back, I probably would have gone crazy," Ruth said with a very tearful tone in her voice.

"I was mighty glad to see you and the canoe as I emerged from the brush," I countered. "I didn't even see anything to shoot. We are out of food, we are going to have to paddle this thing ourselves. I don't dare use the outboard because there is only a little gasoline left in the tank."

We didn't know where the Indians were, nor when they would return, if ever. We decided to wait until morning. If they didn't return by morning, we would leave. We had to, we didn't have anything to eat. Although I had my shotgun, I never saw anything I could shoot. We sure missed Juan.

That night it rained. It was a downpour. Twice in the night I had to get up to bail out the canoe. It rained so hard the coverings over our jungle hammocks couldn't keep out the water. We were soaking wet. When the rain finally stopped, and we got out, we could wring water from our blankets. Everything was wet including our radio/transmitter.

The sun was out, so we put everything out to dry. We didn't have anything to eat, so about noon we decided we had to try to get to Penya Fiel's at Villa Luisa by ourselves. Penya Fiel had a house across the Napo River, the other side of a large island just below the mouth of the Santa Maria.

We prayed and asked for guidance, then shoved off. I sat in the back to paddle and Ruth sat up front to guide the canoe and keep us away from sunken trees.

At this point the river was rather wide, but not flowing much, so we both had to paddle constantly.

Later that afternoon, we arrived at the mouth of the Santa Maria. We floated down the Napo until we got to the far end of the island. I then started the motor to go around the island and up the other side to Penya Fiel's house. About 100 yards from shore, the outboard ran out of gas, but we were able to paddle the rest of the way to shore.

In a very conservative estimate, we figured the motor ran for at least 21 hours—on gasoline that should have taken us only 15 hours. This wasn't the first time God had made something s-t-r-e-t-c-h.

The seventeenth chapter of 1 Kings recounts the story of Elijah and the widow. She had just enough flour and oil for her and her son's last meal. Elijah told her to make a small loaf of bread for him first, and then make one for herself and her son. He told her, "The bowl of flour shall not be exhausted, nor shall the jar of oil be empty, until the day that the Lord sends rain on the face of the earth."

Verse 16 says, "The bowl of flour was not exhausted nor did the jar of oil become empty...."

Hanukkah, the Jewish Feast of Lights, is remembered each year to commemorate the dedication of the second Temple (165 B.C.) at Jerusalem after the first one was destroyed by Antiochus Epiphanes. A lamp burned for eight days from a one-day supply of oil. That's why the Menora has eight candles.

The Book of Mark, chapter 6 says, "And He (Jesus) took the five loaves and the two fish, and looking up toward heaven, He blessed the food and broke the loaves and He kept giving them to the disciples to set before them (the people); and He divided up the two fish among them all. And they all ate and were satisfied."

The same God who fed Elijah, the woman and her son; the God who stretched a one-day's supply of oil into eight; and the One who fed five thousand with five loaves and two fish is the same God who kept the outboard running as long as we needed it.

After tying up the canoe, our first words, after the usual Spanish greeting *"Buenas Tardes,"* were, "Do you have anything to eat? We are starved!"

5 | From the Secoyas to the Orejones

AFTER MAKING ARRANGEMENTS TO STAY AT PENYA Fiel's house, we were given a storage room in which to sleep and store our belongings, and then given a bowl of hot soup. The storage room wasn't much, but at least we could go inside and shut the door—something we hadn't been able to do for over three months.

"Have our things arrived from Iquitos?" I asked the elderly man in charge. Penya Fiel was not at home because he had gone to Iquitos to take a load of goods to sell. He would not be back for several days.

"No, your things are not here, they were dropped off downriver about two hours by boat," was his unconcerned reply.

"They were supposed to have been brought here," I responded.

"The boat your things came on had engine trouble so had to return to Iquitos."

There wasn't anything we could do at the moment about

our supplies, so we said "goodnight" and turned in.

Early the next morning the sun was beating down with its usual tropical fury, so we put the radio in the sun to dry out. We wanted to call the base to let them know we arrived, but we were afraid to try the radio until we were sure it wouldn't short out from the moisture inside.

After a breakfast of more soup, we just sat around, waiting for the radio to dry out. Twenty-two young boys, ranging from 8 to 12 years old, appeared to be getting ready to go to work.

"Who are those boys?" I asked.

"They come here to go to school," the elderly gentleman responded.

My curiosity got the best of me, so I asked, "Why do all of the boys have machetes and are heading for the jungle?"

"To pay for their schooling, they have to work," the old man said.

"When do they go to school, and where is the school house?" I wanted to know.

"They study in the evenings here at this long table."

Our conversation was interrupted when two of the Secoya men who had come down with us silently appeared at the top of the steps. We didn't hear their canoe land, nor did we hear them as they walked up the many steps to the house.

"We want you to take us to Mira Flores so we can walk home," they said in their Secoya language. They were both talking at once.

"I don't have any gasoline. As soon as I get more gasoline, I will take you to Mira Flores," I responded in what I knew of the Secoya language. They seemed to understand.

"The people at the village (where they had left us to go

for a visit) want you to live with them," they said.

That was good news. My response was "*Dea,*" which in Secoya means "good." I told them, again, I would come get them as soon as I had gasoline. I wanted to make sure they understood. With that they left to wait for me at the village.

Later that afternoon, I felt the radio was sufficiently dried out to try. We hooked up the antenna and started the generator.

"Calling Yarina Cocha, calling Yarina Cocha," I blurted into the microphone.

"This is Yarina," was the musical response we wanted to hear.

"Boy, is it ever good to hear your voice!" I answered. "We are at Penya Fiel's on the Napo. We need gasoline for the outboard because we ran out. How soon can you have a plane up here?" I asked.

"We have been wondering where you were, so we have remained on the radio in case you called in. The plane will be in the Iquitos area in about four days so we will bring outboard motor gasoline," the tower operator responded.

The elderly "boss" brought the boys back to the house around five.

While waiting for their supper, they began playing soccer with a ball made from old rags.

With nothing else to do, Ruth and I were watching them. One little boy came over to us and handed each of us a banana. "Don't let anyone see you eating these bananas," the boy said in almost a whisper.

"Why?" was our questioned response.

"We get punished if we are caught stealing food," he said. From personal experience, he knew we weren't getting enough to eat. He was right.

Our soup dinner was served around 6:00 p.m. The adults ate at the long table; the boys ate "downstairs" with the pigs, dogs, and chickens.

As soon as we were finished, the table was cleared and the boys came up for their lesson. A home-made kerosene lamp was placed at each end of the long table—lamps made from small canned milk cans. The lamps were made by punching a hole in the center of the can. The can was then filled with kerosene and a rag stuffed in for the wick. The elderly "teacher" began by having the boys recite the Spanish alphabet. And that was about the extent of their "lesson." After two years, the boys still could not read Spanish. We could not understand why their parents allowed them to work so hard for so little in return.

At around 8:00 p.m., the maid came around with a hot cup of very thick, sweet coffee. It tasted awful, but I drank it so I would not offend them, and I could practice my Spanish. Ruth couldn't stand the taste so excused herself and went to bed.

The house was very large, about 80 feet long and 60 feet wide, set on ironwood posts about 10 feet off the ground, built on the high bank overlooking the mighty Napo River. The twenty crudely made steps rested against the split palm-bark floor, about 10 feet above ground. Most of the house was open except for the small storage room we occupied, the kitchen, another small storage room and a room for Penya Fiel and his mistress. In the middle of the breezeway was the long, narrow dining room table, long enough to seat the twenty-two children. The kitchen stove was a typical jungle stove—a table built on poles, covered with clay on which a fire is kept burning. Everything cooked on it has a distinct smoke flavor.

Penya Fiel was not due back for several days, but he came back early. As he stepped into the house he was rather surprised to see us but gave us a very warm greeting. In our limited Spanish, we gave him a rundown of why we were there and told him about the Indians wanting us to take them up river to Mira Flores so they could walk home, but we were out of gasoline.

"On the way down the Santa Maria River, the Indians left us and went to another village. After two days, I walked back into the jungle to try to find them but couldn't," I explained. "So we came on here by ourselves."

"I have gasoline you can borrow and I know where the village is so I will take you there," he said.

The next morning, Penya Fiel and I left for the village. About an hour's travel up the Santa Maria River we nosed the canoe into the bank at the same spot Ruth and I stopped on the way down. *Senor* Fiel led the way through the jungle to the Indian village. When I had previously gone looking for them, I took the wrong trail. Actually, the village was not very far from the river and we made it there in just a few minutes, but when I went looking for them, I didn't know that.

The village consisted of only two houses, but they appeared to be abandoned. Inside one was a freshly dug grave. It appeared to be that of a small child.

"When a Secoya dies, the Indians bury their dead inside a house and then abandon the village," Penya Fiel told me.

This was very disappointing, because Ruth and I had discussed the possibility of settling among this particular group; especially, since they had expressed an interest in having us live with them.

A well-traveled trail led in a northerly direction. "Let's walk down that trail and see where it leads," I suggested.

We walked for almost five hours down the trail but found nothing. It was getting late and we didn't want to get caught trying to find our way after dark, so we turned around and returned to the houses.

"Would you mind if we waited here until tomorrow to see if they might return?" I asked.

"I don't think they will return, but we can wait until tomorrow if you wish," he responded. He was very congenial.

They had not returned by the morning of the third day, so we decided they were not planning on returning.

We didn't have any idea where the Indians had gone. They may have all decided to return by land to the village up the Santa Maria. That would have been a very difficult trip, but then, they are jungle peoples and used to moving about under a thick canopy of trees, without a compass, unable to see the sky, fording rivers and swamps.

Penya Fiel and I stayed in the village until about noon. Then we decided there was no point in staying any longer, so we returned to Villa Luisa, as his *hacienda* is called. I was very disappointed. I had hoped we could settle with the group near the mouth of the Santa Maria and continue learning their language.

It seemed as though the door to the Secoyas was closing. To borrow a phrase from the movie *The Sound of Music*, when Maria was leaving the Abbey she said, "When the Lord closes a door, somewhere He opens a window." We were now looking for that window. By radio, we talked with our director and explained the entire situation.

Penya Fiel was acquainted with both the Secoyas and the Orejones (who live near the mouth of the Napo) and told us the Secoyas and Orejones speak the same language. He

58

seemed very knowledgeable. We hadn't gotten all that far into the Secoya language, so it didn't really matter. We just wanted to work with an unwritten language—to give them the Bible in their own language. Maybe this was the window we were hoping for.

We relayed this additional information to our director and he suggested we explore the possibility of working among the Orejones.

While waiting for the plane to bring us gasoline, we were hoping the Secoyas would return so I could take them upriver to Mira Flores, but they didn't show up.

The next morning a rather large river boat named the *Aguila* stopped by to sell whatever they could and buy jungle products to sell in Iquitos. Penya Fiel had just returned from Iquitos, so they didn't do much business.

I asked the captain if I could hire him to take our boxes and barrels from the house downriver to the Sucusari River. We agreed on a price, so I tied our 36-foot canoe on behind and left with them, leaving Ruth to follow me later when our plane arrived.

About two hours downriver, the pilot headed for the bank. Under a house set about 300 feet from the river, I could see our boxes and barrels. The boat crew set about carrying our things to the boat. After all was loaded, we headed down the Napo. We stopped at nearly every house along the way to either sell or buy, so we didn't make very good progress. At each stop the boat got heavier and heavier as we loaded on more jungle products. I began to wonder if we would ever get there. To amuse myself, I wrote poetry:

THE AGUILA

The food is good, the water fair, the coffee
    I couldn't drink,
Bellowing cows, and engine noise,
    no human on earth could think.
No place to sit, no place to stand,
    no room to come or go.
The deck was full, the hold was too,
    no chance to go below.
And so I moved from pillar to post,
    in hopes that I could sit,
But then we'd stop and load more on
    and guess just where it lit?
The days were long, the hours slow,
    the minutes, they were too,
Just how many days will it take this tub
    before this trip is through?
Four more days the Captain says will get us
    there if nothing does go wrong,
But then he says, "I'm not real sure
    just how long."
So I grit my teeth and pray for grace,
    then on and on we go.
Steam engines run, they work just fine,
    but man they sure are slow.

There wasn't much to do except watch the river bank slip slowly by. Occasionally, we saw a monkey or two swing from branch to branch looking for food. Groups of colorful macaws flew lazily by, their plumage glistening gold and blue.

I had lots of time to think and reflect. As I thought about our recent past and our inability to work among the Secoyas, the following came to mind:

It seems I've lived a long, long time
    and accomplished oh so little.
It seems that all I ever do is sit
    around and piddle.
I wish I could get down to work
    and do a little good.
If I just had the solution,
    I'm sure I really would.
There are so many problems I don't
    know how to handle,
I get confused and frustrated before
    I'm really in the saddle.
I've thought it through and know
    I've got ambition
But to get to work kinda bothers me,
    Maybe I should have gone a fishin.

Eight long days later the captain headed for the mouth of the Sucusari River. "Here is where you get off," he informed me.

Just to the south of the mouth of the Sucusari, set on a hill overlooking the Napo, was the rather large grass-roofed house of Rosario Rios. Typical of all the jungle houses, it consisted of a palm-bark floor set on ironwood posts about 4 feet off the ground. In the far left corner was a small bedroom for the *Senora*. The rest was the unwalled open sitting area. An Indian hammock was strung between two of the upright posts. An old Singer sewing machine sat against the wall of one room. To the east was a separate hut for the fire table. A short walkway connected the two buildings.

As I entered the house I greeted the elderly lady, "Good afternoon, my name is Roberto. I understand the Orejon Indians live up the Sucusari River. My wife and I would like to live among them and learn their language. Do you think that would be possible?"

"Good afternoon. I am *Senora* Rios. I am the owner of the Indians. I don't think it would be a good idea to live among them, because they are gone much of the time. They work for me and I send them off to work. But you can live near me and I will provide an Indian to teach you their language," she offered.

Although she agreed to help us, I had an uneasy feeling that she really didn't want us "messing" with "her" Indians.

"Thanks, that would be fine," I said. "Would you mind if I store our things under your house until my wife and I come out to begin working on the language? First, though, we feel we need to learn more Spanish and have arranged to go to Lima for study. We should be back in a couple of months," I told her.

Underneath her house was open, so our things would be protected from the tropical rains.

She agreed that would be OK, so the boat crew unloaded our things and put them under the house. I paid the captain and settled in to await Ruth and the plane from Villa Luisa.

Don Benigno Pinedo nosed his canoe into shore just below the house. As he walked toward the house he stopped to look at the boxes and barrels stored under the house.

"Good afternoon," he said as he extended his hand; a puzzled look shrouded his suntanned face. "I am Benigno

Pinedo," he said in jungle Spanish (a sing-song Spanish not well understood in Lima).

"This is my husband," *Senora* Rosario ventured.

"My name is Roberto. My wife and I are linguists and wish to learn the Orejon language. The *Senora* says we can live near here and she will provide an Orejon to teach us their language. Could I hire you to build us a house?" I asked.

"Of course, I would be happy to build you a house," he said.

"How much will you charge to build a house?" I asked.

"I can build you a nice house for 900 *soles* (about $130)," he said. That sounded reasonable to me so we agreed on the price and shook hands.

"I will need some money to pay the helpers," *Don* Benigno informed me.

"How much will you need?" I asked.

"Four hundred *soles* would be enough," he said. I paid him the 400.

"My wife and I have to go to Lima for a couple of months. Could you have the house ready for us when we get back?" I asked.

"No problem. I know of two other men I can get to help me. It will be ready."

The next question was the location. The *Senora* wanted him to build the house next to hers. However, there really wasn't a very good spot because a swamp occupied the area between her house and the Sucusari River.

"Ruth will be here in a day or two. Let's let her help us decide the best place," I suggested.

Two days later the plane splashed down in front of the house. As Ruth and the pilot stepped from the plane, I introduced them to the *Senora* and to *Don* Benigno. Their "pleased to meet you," did not have a ring of sincerity to it.

The pilot took off immediately because he was having trouble with the plane's engine and needed to get back to Yarina. As we stood watching the small plane disappear over the horizon, that same sense of loneliness swept over both of us.

"The *Senora* wants to build our house over there," I said as I pointed to a spot a short distance behind the *Senora's*. "What do you think?"

"Let's not decide today," she responded. "It looks as though we are going to be here for a few days anyway. Let's take a walk around and see what we can find. Right now, I would like something to eat."

The next morning, we decided to take a walk around the area and see if we could find a better spot for a house. The swamp covered a large area just below the house and extending some distance back. However, a narrow strip next to the river was slightly raised, and dry. A trail led along the bank next to the Sucusari. We followed the trail as it wound back and forth among the trees. Soon it began to climb to a beautiful spot overlooking the Sucusari River, a short distance from the mouth.

"Let's have the house built here," Ruth ventured.

"This looks like a very nice spot. And we can get to know the Indians as they come down the river," I responded.

"*Senora*, we have found a nice spot for a house, and we would like to have it built there. Come, let us show you." *Senora*, *Don* Benigno, Ruth, and I took a short walk to the spot.

"See, this is a beautiful spot. What do you think?" we asked with a little exuberance in our voices.

"Let's go back to the house and talk about it," the *Senora* suggested.

There was much discussion about the location of the house, but Ruth and I held out for "our"spot and finally won out.

"Good, that's settled," I said. "And, *Don* Benigno, the house will be ready for us when we return, right?"

"No problem, it will be ready."

By radio we learned another plane would be in Iquitos in about four days, but they would not be stopping by for us. We had to find another way to Iquitos. We didn't see a problem with that as *albarengas* were constantly coming and going from Iquitos. We just needed to flag one down.

Just below the *Senora's* was a large island in the middle of the Napo. Below the island, the river curved sharply to the east. But to the north, the river was straight and we could see for a long distance before the river made another sharp curve.

Unless one is ill, nobody sleeps late in the jungle. As soon as the darkness begins to lighten, everyone is up and moving about. Ruth and I ate a quick breakfast of rice and fish, and then began looking for a boat going to Iquitos. It wasn't long before we spotted a loaded *albarenga* plowing its way toward us. We ran down to the river's edge and began waving for him to stop.

"We need to get to Iquitos. Can you take us?" we asked.

"Hop on," the man who appeared to be in charge said.

"How much?" I asked.

"Thirty *soles*," was his reply. We paid him the thirty soles ($4.00) and climbed aboard. Three days later we were in Iquitos—the same day the plane arrived.

It was wonderful to get back to Yarina and be able to

speak English again. At the church service Sunday morning, we gave our report of the past three plus months—a rather discouraging report of troubles and trials. The next day we headed by National Airlines (Faucett) on to Lima for Spanish study and a much-needed rest. We were tired.

6 | Spanish Study in Lima

"WHILE YOU ARE IN LIMA, I WANT YOU TO GET REST-ed up. I know you have had a difficult time trying to get settled in a language situation. Tell me, how do you feel about returning to the Orejones?" Uncle Cam questioned.

"We want to go back. But we do need more Spanish. We can get along with what we have, but it would be much better if we were more fluent," we said.

"Do you think the *Senora* will cooperate with you?" Uncle Cam queried.

"We didn't have a good feeling about our 'messing' with 'her' Indians. It bothered me when she said 'my Indians.' She was somewhat cordial, but we had the feeling she would have been happier if we hadn't come," we answered.

"Well, you go on into Lima and get some more Spanish and when you return I will send someone with you to help you get settled and to evaluate the situation," Uncle Cam continued. "While in Lima, you will be expected to attend Spanish classes and to live with a Peruvian family so you will get immersed in the language. The director in Lima will arrange all this for you."

For the time being we were living with a family at the base awaiting the plane trip to Lima. The next day we were driven over the bumpy road to the airport.

Flying over the vast carpet of green jungle and then climbing up, up and over the majestic Andes Mountains is breathtaking. As we approached the mountains, I went into the pilots' cabin so I could get a full view of the mountains. As I was filming, the Captain said, "Would you like a better view?" With that he banked the plane and circled over the shimmering blue glacier lakes that dot the tops of the mountains. I got some marvelous pictures. However, I'm not sure the passengers were all that thrilled about circling just above the jagged mountain peaks.

Once again Grandma Cudney met us at the airport with her usual bouquet of flowers. Lima is a city of flowers— beautiful red and purple bougainvillea splashed against walls and houses.

"Welcome once again to Lima. We have a room already reserved for you until you get assigned to a Peruvian home," Mrs. Cudney said with her usual exuberance.

"After more than three months in a very isolated situation, it's going to take a few days to get used to being back in civilization. It will be nice to speak English again with women of my own culture," Ruth said.

"We have been praying for the two of you, having heard of the problems you had getting into the tribe," Mrs. Cudney continued. "The station wagon is parked out front. We can talk on the way to the group house."

Our Assignment

We were assigned to live in a lovely home on the palm studded avenue Arequipa leading to the exclusive area called Miraflores. At one time the lady was rather affluent. However, her husband had passed away and she was still trying to keep up the upper-crust front, but not doing it very well.

She was struggling financially. This is why she was taking in boarders—us and another young missionary couple also there to learn Spanish. We were supposed to be provided with meals so we could converse around the table. Unfortunately, the family rarely ate with us. Worse still, we weren't getting enough to eat. The lady had a young Inca Indian maid working for her. For every meal she sent the woman to the market to buy just enough for that particular meal, but didn't give her enough money. Consequently, we had to supplement our meager diet at the local corner store.

We later learned the reason. Her daughter was about to come of age, entering adulthood, and the lady needed money to finance the coming-out party. We were paying for it with the food she wasn't buying.

Finally, we couldn't take it any more. We were all losing weight when we needed to be gaining weight from our jungle diet, so we made an appointment with our director.

"We can't keep living in the *Senora's* house," we informed him.

"What's the problem?"

"There are two problems. We are not getting enough to eat for one thing, and, the *Senora's* daughter keeps the radio blaring full-blast all day long, so we are unable to concentrate to study."

"OK, I'll talk with the *Senora* and see what can be done," was the best the director could do at the time.

After he talked with the *Senora*, the only thing that changed was the *Senora's* attitude toward us. She became very cool. After another week, we decided the situation wasn't getting any better so we took things into our own hands. We found an apartment where we could house-sit while the couple went on vacation. We informed our director we were moving because we couldn't continue living with the *Senora* and her daughter.

If the jungle base at Yarina Cocha was the hub of the work, Lima was the nerve center. The Institute's offices were in the building that housed the Ministry of Education (under whom the organization operated), the office of the purchasing agent (known as "the buyer"), and the group home. The office handled visas for the members, and the general finances, and kept in close touch with the Ministry of Education. The buyer's office kept the base supplied with whatever it needed that could be purchased in Lima and transshipped via trucks across the rugged Andes Mountains over a very treacherous road. And the group home was the "hotel" that fed and housed the members and friends as they came and went from Lima.

In the apartment we were able to invite our new Peruvian friends for dinner so we could practice our Spanish. Going to the market every day gave Ruth an opportunity to "haggle" over prices and thereby gain more practice. One did not haggle over prices in most stores, but at the open markets it was a ritual. Everyone haggled to get the best price, something that was expected. The seller wanted to get the most he could, and the buyer wanted to get the best buy he could. It was not only interesting but fun to try for the rock-bottom price. Of course, as *Gringos*, the beginning price was always quoted much higher for us than for the nationals. And, I am sure the final price we paid was higher than for the nationals, but we got a lot of Spanish practice and made a lot of friends.

Peru is divided into three distinct areas: the arid coastal plain, the Andes mountains, and the jungle. It rains in Lima only about once in every twenty-five years, and then only a slight drizzle. Consequently, houses are not built to keep out the rain. Most houses are constructed of cement, bricks, or adobe with the usual big city slums which are made of whatever materials that can be scrounged.

There were no public bathrooms which created another problem. Vacant lots, surrounded by 10-foot-high adobe walls, were used as emergency bathrooms. The walls were constructed without doors, but if one had an urgent need, he or she made a door. If an urgent need presented itself and there were no vacant lots near by, a tree or bush served the same purpose. And because it doesn't rain to wash away the excrement, the smell is less than pleasant.

A visitor was asked what impressed her about Lima. "Ten thousand people urinating on the streets," was her answer.

Peru contains a wealth of natural resources. The ocean teems with fish which feed the *guano* birds. Just off the coast of Peru are the Chincha Islands, the small islands that harbor the *guano* birds. *Guano* is the term for the droppings of sea birds; hence, the term *guano* birds because of the large amount of droppings they produce on the tiny islands. *Guano* is an excellent fertilizer that is harvested and exported world-wide, as well as used locally.

Gold and silver has been mined in the Andes Mountains

since before the discovery of Peru by the white man. The story is told of an Inca Indian who stopped to build a fire to cook his meal. When the fire got hot, gold began to flow from the fire.

The Irish potato did not originally come from Ireland, but from Peru. There are over 3,000 varieties of potatoes grown in Peru. The Incas used freeze-drying to preserve potatoes long before we "invented" the process.

The coastal plain is dry and arid, but once it is watered, it blossoms like a rose. The ground is very fertile and produces abundant fruits, vegetables, and melons, aided, I am sure, by the guano fertilizer.

The jungle is rich in mahogany, wild pig skins (peccary), jungle rubber (latex), jungle nuts, and tropical fruits, especially bananas. Until I went to South America, I never thought about what footballs were made of. They are not made from the skins of domestic pigs, but from the skins of wild pigs, the peccary. It didn't even dawn on me that, when I purchased a slab of bacon, the skin from the pig was attached. Wild pig skins are made into footballs, shoes, belts, and other items requiring leather.

Being south of the Equator, Peru's seasons are the reverse of ours. I used to get amused at Santa Claus, during the Christmas season in Peru, dressed in his red suit, sweat pouring off his chin as he stood in the hot sunshine saying "Ho! Ho! Ho!"

7 | A Blowtorch and a Little Knowledge

THREE MONTHS OF SPANISH STUDY IN LIMA DID NOT make us native speakers, but it did give us enough basics to build upon. I am sure we still butchered the grammar, but at least we did better than "pidgin" Spanish.

When we returned to Yarina Cocha, we were told of a large group of Secoyas living in Ecuador who could be reached better from there. Also, this group lives on the shore of a large lake where our float planes can land, making access to them much easier.

Another couple had already been assigned to work with them so we were free to concentrate on working among the Orejones. Now we understood why the door to the Secoyas had closed for us and the window to the Orejones opened.

Because our supplies were now at Rosario Rios, we only needed to take along staples: rice, flour, sugar, etc. Besides, we would only be a day and a half by outboard from Iquitos. We did, however, need an outboard motor, but we didn't have money to buy one.

Under a bench at the hangar at Yarina, I discovered a 1928 Johnson outboard. However, it wasn't all there—the housing from the power unit to the propeller unit was missing. With the aid of the airplane mechanic, Ernest Rich, we made the necessary housing from a 2-inch water pipe. We put the old Johnson together and it worked just fine. It was big and heavy, but it ran.

Soon we were ready to return to the Sucusari to begin working among the Orejones. We were "experienced" now in living in primitive conditions, so we packed only the things we knew we would need and loaded everything into the larger Catalina Flying Boat. While in Lima, we were able to purchase a foam rubber mattress. We were tired of sleeping on hard *pona* (palm bark) floors. We also purchased a small 2 1/2 cu. ft. kerosene refrigerator for use in the tribe— not only for storing food, but also for storing vials of antibiotics which we knew we would be needing.

After a round of prayers by those who came to see us off, we taxied down the lake and were soon airborne, headed for Iquitos and on to our house near the mouth of the Sucusari.

The plane glided noiselessly to shore as the pilot cut the engines. The *Senora* did not come down to greet us as was the usual custom, but remained in her house, looking down at us. I got the feeling she was not happy to see us.

Don Benigno, however, did come down and greeted us.

"You have been gone a long time," he said.

"Good afternoon, *Don* Benigno. Yes, we stayed in Lima longer than we had planned, but our time was well spent. We know more Spanish now," I said with a slight chuckle. "By the way, is our house ready?"

"I am very sorry, but I have not been able to get the

other men to help me." He must have seen the look of disappointment on my face so he continued. "Don't worry, we will get it built, the other men will be free soon to help me. We will start next Monday."

Ruth and I walked up to the house to greet the *Senora*.

"Good afternoon, *Senora* Rios. We have finally returned, but *Don* Benigno tells us the house is not built. Could we occupy a corner of your house until ours is built?" we asked.

"Good afternoon. Yes, you may put your things over there," as she pointed to the river-front corner of the house which did give us a nice view of the river and a view of the comings and goings up and down the river.

A very young, attractive lady was standing in the background. The *Senora* motioned for her to come forward.

"This is my son Herman's wife, Aurora," she informed us. Herman was her son who usually accompanied the Indians when they were sent to work gathering wild rubber milk or to cut rosewood. He was away with the Indians at the time. We extended our hand and greeted her. She appeared very reserved, rather subdued. She looked like a whipped puppy. We soon learned, she may have been Herman's wife, but she was the *Senora's* maid.

As soon as all our things were brought into the house, the plane left us and we were again on our own. The pilot later recalled that as he pulled away and waved to us, we looked awfully forlorn. "You looked as though you were about to cry," he said.

"I don't think we were about to cry, but I will have to admit, we were sad to see you leave us; left to again fend for ourselves," I answered.

Monday came and went. Tuesday, Wednesday, Thursday, Friday, Saturday, and Sunday came and went. Still no progress on the house. Even *Don* Benigno was gone.

"Where is *Don* Benigno?" I finally asked.

"He had to take my Indians off to work," the *Senora* said with that same tone of finality. There was that word again, "my Indians." She seemed to delight in emphasizing the "my Indians." "*Don* Benigno will be back soon," she said with a somewhat "What's the difference?" attitude.

"He promised me he would have our house completed," I said with a rather agitated tone in my voice.

She just walked away.

We had our own food, so we were not expecting her to feed us. However, we did not feel right eating our food in front of her so shared our food with her and Aurora. We soon got the feeling she was enjoying our American food. This was putting quite a drain on our own food supply.

However, it didn't take long for news to spread along the Napo River that two *Gringos* were living at the *Senora's* house. Soon we had visitors. Most of them brought gifts of bananas, cassava root, eggs, and fish, which helped to supplement our food supply. In return we gave them fish hooks, mirrors, and other trade goods items. There were no stores in the area, so anything we gave them was more than they had before. Apparently, they hadn't seen many North Americans, so we were a curiosity.

Finally *Don* Benigno came back.

"When will you get our house built?" we asked.

"Very soon. We will start on it right away."

Another week passed—no house.

The strain of not getting things moving and having to live out of boxes and barrels was getting to us. The lack of privacy was probably the worst inconvenience.

Our "American" way of having things done on schedule

reared its ugly head and I blew up. "You have been deceiving us! You don't intend to build us a house!" I said in a raised voice.

Senora Rios became very angry. For a while, I thought she was going to order us out of her house and I had no idea where we would go.

This, though, was the turning point. Her attitude changed and she ordered *Don* Benigno to begin working on the house.

Even though he got started, progress was still very slow. Although I had given *Don* Benigno 400 *soles*, he did not hire anyone to help. I suppose he wanted all the money for himself. At any rate he began slowly gathering the materials for the house. Ironwood posts had to be located and brought in from the jungle. Ironwood is the heart of certain trees that are blown down by strong winds. The outer wood rots away leaving the very hard heart of the tree. They are very heavy and termite-proof.

He began gathering materials around the first of July. By the middle of August he hadn't even started the construction. To further save money, they brought down some of the Orejones to help. This gave me good opportunity to get to know them and gain their confidence.

Progress was very slow. If *Don* Benigno decided to go somewhere, all work stopped. Nearly three months had slipped by since we had returned from Lima. We were getting weary.

After the Indians wove the palm fronds onto long poles for the roof and had the roof on, the *Senora* paid them—five bottles of whiskey.

"We don't want this, but she makes us take it," one of the Indians told me. "We don't like her." I had learned enough of the Secoya language to communicate somewhat with the Orejones. I think this further bothered the *Senora*.

To keep busy, Ruth helped the *Senora* sew clothing for the Indians. Ruth is a professional seamstress, but the *Senora* said to her, "You don't sew very well." Ruth tried to sew nice dresses, but all the *Senora* wanted was a long piece of cloth, folded and sewn up both sides, leaving room for the head and arms. Sewing sleeves and neck yokes would take too much material and time.

By the end of August the house was nearly completed except for the palm-bark floor. Being anxious to get moved out of the *Senora's* house and into our own place, I went up the Napo looking for men. I had no trouble finding workers. They would have come to help *Don* Benigno, too, but I was told, "The *Senora* won't pay us, and the food she serves is too little and terrible. We can't work on so little food."

"If I pay you five *soles* a day, will you work for me?"

"For five *soles* a day, I can get all the help you need."

Don Enrique rounded up six men to cut the pona (palm trees) for the floor. In two days it was completed at a cost of only sixty *soles*.

Next, I walled off two-thirds of the house for our living quarters. We were now ready to move into our new home— and finally have some privacy.

We thanked the *Senora* for her hospitality, gave her a nice gift and began transferring our things. But first I had to make steps from the river to the house—forty-five of them up a rather steep bank. At the foot of the steps a large log extended into the river making a nice dock. After I finished the steps, we hired men to bring our boxes from under the *Senora's* house.

As the men wrestled the 200-pound box of tools I had "thrown" in, I kept wondering why I had brought them along. I was soon to learn why.

We tried to make the house as much a home as possible. Ruth has always loved gardening, so we spaded up a small plot for a garden and she planted the seeds sent from America, but the leaf cutting ants cut off the sprouts as soon as they poked their heads above ground. We finally gave that up as a lost cause. Later though, we were able to control the leaf-cutting ants, also called parasol ants, by sprinkling arsenic on the leaves. The ants carried the leaves to their nest and the arsenic did the rest.

Although these ants are destructive little rascals, they are interesting. Their 2-inch-wide trail crossed our path that led to the river. All night long a steady stream of ants kept very busy coming and going to and from their nest somewhere underground. As the ants cut pieces from a leaf, they carried the dime-sized pieces between their pincers to their nest. The pieces of leaves looked like little green sails.

Once in the nest, other ants chewed the leaves into a mass and carried the mass to the ant garden in another part of the nest. This mass is used as fertilizer to feed their mushroom garden, their only source of food.

We were able to buy chickens from the folks living along the Napo River. Eggs were very scare because the Peruvians only used the eggs for setting; they didn't eat them. We wanted fresh eggs to eat. Whenever we did buy eggs, they often had unhatched baby chicks inside. I decided to build a chicken house for our own chickens. I was busy cutting poles for our new chicken house when a Peruvian came by. "*Senor,* you must cut the poles according to the moon otherwise the termites will eat them." I thanked him for his advice and continued cutting poles. *Just a silly superstition*, I told myself. I built the little chicken house, and it looked pretty good for someone who had only built a pole house during our training in Mexico. The termites thought so, too—they ate it just like they did our house in Mexico. From then on I listened to our neighbors.

Our relationship with the *Senora* and her daughter-in-law was very good. At least on the outside. She even sent food over for us. We always thanked her profusely, but we never ate it. The Peruvians who came to visit us warned us she might poison the food. She may not have, but we weren't taking any chances.

After we were pretty well settled in our new home, I asked the *Senora*, "Would it be OK if I went to the Indians' village just to visit?"

"Of course," was her quick reply. "I will go with you." We all climbed into my big 36-foot canoe and headed up the Sucusari. The river was full of water so it only took us two hours to get there. The old Johnson ran well.

As we nudged the canoe to the bank, three of the Orejon men were standing on the high bank leading to the house. A wide, slippery path led up the steep incline.

We greeted the men but received no response. We all walked over to the house and climbed the notched pole. Inside was Miguel's elderly wife, Maria, their daughter, Isidora, and her husband, Daniel, and their two children, Irisi, about ten, and Mateo, about eight, and Hilario, the prospective son-in-law.

The *Senora* told us Hilario had asked Isidora and Daniel for their daughter Irisi to be his wife. We learned later, it is their custom for the prospective son-in-law to prove himself by living in the home to prove he would be a good husband.

Hilario was made to carry the water, supply the firewood, help in planting the cassava root garden, hunt for meat for the household, and do any other chores required of him. He was the family "slave" until the family accepted him, only then was Hilario allowed to marry Irisi.

I also learned it is not their custom to greet when someone arrives. Not until the person has been there for several minutes do they speak. Everyone sits quietly. Finally, after a period of silence, the oldest man of the house will ask, "Would he like something to eat?"

In this case, Miguel asked the *Senora* if I would like something to eat. They never asked a direct question. Whenever they asked me for something, the person would say, "My wife would like some fishhooks." The wife would then respond, "My husband would like some, too."

Although their houses are as large as the Secoyas, they are built similar to the Peruvians living along the Napo. The palm-bark floor is 4 to 5 feet off the ground with no walls or partitions. A notched log allows entry into the house. At night, the log is pulled into the house to keep out the animals.

We soon understood why the *Senora* was so eager to accompany us to the village. She wanted cassava roots and ordered the women to dig two large baskets for her to take home. The men also had several peccary (wild pig) skins which she took. She didn't pay them anything. They gave her whatever she asked for. We began to see why she was not happy to have us living among them. The Indians were her slaves, and she wanted to keep them that way.

The communal house was loosely divided into sections. A small space for each family. They didn't own much: a few pieces of well-worn clothing, a small wooden footlocker-type box in which they kept their "things." Three large hand-woven hammocks stretched between the house poles. These were their beds. The entire family slept in a single, large hammock, the same as the Secoyas. Long blowguns hung from the roof poles, and several canoe paddles were stuck into the grass roof. The only place for me to sit was on an old, upturned canoe. The people sat on their haunches—their culture didn't call for chairs.

A fire table stood at the far end of the building. Several pieces of wild pig was being smoke-cured on a pole rack above the fire, the smoke from the smoldering fire curled upward around the meat keeping away the flies.

After being served a piece of the smoked wild pig, I said to Miguel who spoke quite a bit of Spanish, "I would like to learn your language."

"I can teach you," he said without giving the matter a second thought.

The *Senora* was eyeing me with suspicion, wondering what I was up to. She cut our conversation short by saying, "We need to leave."

I didn't learn until later there were other Orejon houses a short distance up the river. The chief's house was about thirty minutes by paddle. Gustavo's house was another twenty minutes.

Miguel was the only one who spoke much Spanish. When we were finally able to live among them, he told me his story. When he was a boy, a renegade Peruvian army general wanted to take over the country and began by forming a rag-tag army. Miguel was captured and put in his army. It was during this period of time he learned some Spanish. We were told the general was defeated and executed and Miguel was free to return to his home.

We loaded the baskets of cassava roots and the skins into the canoe and left. The river was flowing quite rapidly, so it didn't take us long to get home.

"I don't think the *Senora* has any intention of providing us with an Orejon to teach us. After we gain their confidence, maybe we can live in the village. Did I tell you what one of the Orejon men weaving the shingles for our roof told me?"

"No, you didn't," Ruth responded.

"He told me in his very limited Spanish, 'No like *Senora*. No want *aguardiente'* (the sugarcane whiskey). For all the work they do for her she pays them very little. I just hope we can eventually help them obtain their freedom. I can't understand the hold the *Senora* has over them," I commented.

We continued living near the mouth of the Sucusari. We never lacked for visitors. As soon as the Peruvians living along the Napo heard we were living near the mouth, they began arriving. This gave us a lot of opportunities to practice our Spanish. Most of them came because they wanted something: shotgun shells, fish hooks, medicines, or to repair outboard motors. We didn't mind, because we were there to serve and we enjoyed their visits.

One fellow we named (in English) "half asleep," because that is what he kept telling us, "*Estoy medio dormicido.*" He came to us to cure him of his leprosy. Unfortunately the leprosy was in its advanced stages. He didn't have long to live and there wasn't anything we could do for him.

"If you will cure me, I will pay you," he kept telling us.

One day he was carried up the forty-five steps with a plea for help. We didn't want to tell him there wasn't anything we could do for him, so I gave him a shot of plain distilled water and sent him away with a handful of yeast tablets. "Take three of these a day," I told him.

A few days later, he walked on his own up the forty-five steps that led to our house and said, "That was good medicine you gave me. Could you give me some more? As soon as I am cured I will pay you." I gave him another shot of distilled water and another handful of yeast tables.

He was a frequent visitor until he was admitted to a leprosarium down the Amazon River. He died a few weeks later.

The next day, three of the Orejon men stopped at our house on the way to the *Senora's*. They were taking several wild pig skins to her. After dropping off the skins, they again stopped by on their way home.

"What did the *Senora* give you for the skins?" I asked.

They showed me a liter bottle of kerosene and two half-liter bottles of *aguardiente*, literally "fire water" in Spanish. The pig skins were worth twenty-nine *soles* each (about $4 U.S.) What she gave them was worth about one *sole*. We were more certain than ever why we weren't wanted by the *Senora*.

The men wanted fishhooks. Following their custom, they asked, "He wants some fishhooks." The other repeated, "He wants some, too." We gave them all several fishhooks. As they left, one of them said, "*Senora* bad."

The following morning, we went to visit the *Senora*. In the course of the conversation, I asked, "When are you going to give us one of the Orejones so we can learn their language as you promised?"

"I don't know, I will have to think about it," she responded.

Days turned into weeks; still no Indians. I did manage to go to the village occasionally, after a heavy rain when the river was high enough for me to make it with my big canoe. Miguel was always happy to give me words to write down.

Each time I went, I took along lots of medicine. On one of the trips, a young boy had large infected sores all over his body, and high fever. I gave him a shot of antibiotics with the promise I would continue to treat him. Every day for several days I returned to treat the boy. This went a long way to gaining their confidence. Each time, I wrote down more Orejon words and expressions. I was slowly getting into the language and became convinced the Orejones and the Secoyas spoke the same language—just different dialects. Many of their words and expressions were very close.

Each time I went, more sick and injured were brought to me. I became a "miracle worker"—thanks to our United States antibiotics and aspirin supply. The boy completely recovered.

It wasn't long before more Peruvians found out I could repair outboard engines. This wasn't what I had in mind when I brought along my tools. But then, I guess I really didn't know why I brought them along.

Late one afternoon, a man came walking up to our house. "My name is *Senor* Godoy. The *Senora* told me you were living here so I came to visit." We sat and talked for about half an hour when he said, "By the way, my outboard motor broke down in front of the *Senora's* house. Do you suppose you could fix it?"

"Bring it to the house and let me look at it," I answered.

His outboard was a 10 h.p. Swedish Penta—a popular motor used to push heavy cargo up and down the rivers.

I checked the spark and there wasn't any. "Your problem is electrical," I told him.

"Can you fix it?" he asked.

"I don't know," I responded. "But let's take the fly wheel off and take a look."

I took the flywheel off and immediately saw the problem. The wire from the coil to the condenser had come off the coil. Now I knew why I had taken along the blowtorch and soldering supplies. I immediately heated up the soldering iron and soldered the wire back on, put the motor back together, and—presto! We had spark.

Since it was late in the afternoon, we asked *Senor* Godoy if he would like to stay for dinner. He accepted.

During dinner he said, "I can't understand why you young people left your comfortable homes in the United States to live out here."

"We are linguists, and we are also Christians. We are here because we feel God wants us to translate the Bible into the language of the Orejones."

"I am the *patron* (protector) of the Arabela Indians. In fact, I am on my way to the Arabela village up the Curaray River now. Do you suppose someone could come and work with the Arabelas?" he ventured.

Now we knew for certain why I brought along my tools. Mr. Godoy could have broken down anywhere along the river, but he didn't. He broke down in front of our place. Was that pure coincidence?

"We will call our base and ask if someone is available to work with the Arabelas," we told him.

Early the next morning he was off to trade with the Arabelas. Before he left, however, we called Yarina Cocha by radio and *Senor* Godoy was able to talk personally with Mr. Townsend, our director. A young couple had just arrived from the United States who he felt would be just the ones for the job.

A little knowledge of mechanics and a blowtorch opened the door to another tribe. A tribe which now has the *New Testament* in its own language, a school where the children are learning to read and write, and a church where they can gather to worship. A whole new world opened up for them.

8 | We Were Supposed to Die

THE ONLY CONTACT WE WERE HAVING WITH THE Orejones were the times I went to the village (when the river was high enough), or the times they came down the river. It was obvious the *Senora* was not going to provide someone to teach us the language, because we had already spent a year trying to get to where we could work with them. The *Senora* would make a promise, then renege on her promise.

We could relate to what Paul wrote in his letter to the Roman Church. In Romans 15:21-22, he wrote: "but as it is written, they who had no news of Him shall see, and they who have not heard shall understand. For this reason I have often been hindered from coming to you."

It seemed evident Satan did not want us invading his territory and he was doing everything possible to keep us from giving God's Word to the Orejones.

The *Senora* and we both knew that when the Indians began learning, they would figure out she had been cheating them, and she didn't want that. She wanted them kept in ignorance so she could continue exploiting them.

The *Prefect* (mayor) of the area lived about a half day by outboard up the Napo. We decided we should make the trip to pay him a visit and see what he could do to convince the *Senora* to provide us with someone to teach us the language.

We left very early in order to make it there and back in one day. There was no way to communicate with him other than in person, and we just hoped he would be there. We knew he spent a lot of his time in Iquitos.

Fortunately, he was at home and we were able to present our problem to him. He was very cordial and said he would come down and have a talk with the *Senora.*

A day or two later he did show up. However, his talk with the *Senora* was fruitless.

"How can you deal with a woman like that?" he commented.

"Tell you what. There is another Orejon family living at Urco Miranyo, about two hours by outboard up the Napo. They work for *Senor* Flores. Talk with him and see if you can work with his Indians," the Mayor suggested. There was "his Indians" again.

In the year we had been at the Sucusari, no one ever told us there was another Orejon family living up the Napo. *Why would God allow us to waste a year just sitting?* we wondered. Well, it wasn't really wasted. Had we not been there, we would not have located the Arabela Indians. And I did make progress in the language. I was memorizing words and phrases. And we did get acquainted with the Orejones living up the Sucusari which was a big help when we finally did get to live among them.

We took the two-hour trip up the Napo to Miranyo. *Senor* Flores was at home and welcomed us. He knew about us and he knew the problems we were having with the *Senora* because news traveled fast up and down the Napo. They didn't have telephones, but they did have the system of "tell-someone."

"Good afternoon, *Senor* Flores. The *Prefect* told me you have an Orejon family working for you."

"Yes, I do," he responded. "The *Prefect* has already talked with me about your coming up here to learn the Orejon language," he said. "You are most welcome."

"I don't have any place for you to live, so we will have to move your house up here. Come, let me show you a good place to put it," he suggested.

The Indians were not there at the time because they were away working for Mr. Flores. Their small house was about 100 meters below Mr. Flores' house. He suggested we move our house near theirs so we could be close to them.

"Not another move," Ruth said with a disappointed tone in her voice.

"If we are going to live here and learn the language, I guess we will have to," I said.

We thanked Mr. Flores and returned to the Sucusari.

The next day, Miguel staggered up to our house. He was very drunk, too drunk to paddle home, so he stayed at our place until he sobered up.

"Where did you get the *aguardiente*?" I asked Miguel.

"I took dried wild pig skins to the *Senora's* and she gave me five bottles of *aguardiente*. I didn't want them, but she made me take them. She says I still owe her," he said in a very slurred voice.

"What else did she give you?" I asked.

91

"A bar of soap," he said.

I could see what the *Senora* was trying to do. She was trying to get them hooked on alcohol. I then did something that could have caused a serious problem. I poured out the remaining bottles of liquor.

"Why did you pour out the *aguardiente*?" Miguel asked.

"Because I don't want you drinking anymore. I will buy them from you," I said as I handed him several items I knew he would like and which were much more valuable than the cheap liquor.

I didn't know what his reaction would be. But after a period of silence, while he looked at the things I had given him, he said, "You did the right thing. *Aguardiente* is bad. I don't like the *Senora*, I don't want to work for her anymore."

He then took two shotgun shells from his pocket and said, "The *Senora* gave me these to kill you. But I won't kill you."

Finally, Miguel was sober enough to paddle the canoe to his village and left.

Two days later he came back to our house. "Maria is very sick, and the *Senora* won't help her. Can you come and cure her?" he pleaded.

"Of course," I said, as I picked up our medical kit. Miguel tied his canoe on behind my bigger canoe and we took off for the two-hour trip to the village.

I could see Maria was very ill with a temperature of 103°F. I gave her a shot of penicillin and returned home after telling Miguel I would talk with our doctor and be back in the morning.

The doctor told me to continue giving her the series of penicillin shots and to start her on sulfa.

The next morning Maria was worse. Her temperature was 105°F. I remained there the entire day treating her.

When I talked with the doctor by radio he told me there wasn't much hope for Maria with a temperature of 105°F. There wasn't anything more we could do except pray.

We didn't want to lose Maria, not only because she had become very dear to us, but also because she was the catalyst that kept the family unit together.

The Orejon family unit revolves around the grandmother. Their culture is matriarchal. When the grandmother dies, the family unit is broken up and each child then begins another family unit.

The next morning as I talked by radio to the base, I requested prayer for Maria. Ruth and I had a time of prayer for her, then left for the village.

From what the doctor told us, we didn't expect Maria to be alive. I guess our faith was too small, but as we rounded the bend to the house, we could see Maria sitting up. She was weak, but very much alive and her fever was down. We continued administering the penicillin and sulfa. We also treated several of the children for eye infections. As we left that evening, we gave Miguel enough sulfa, with instructions, to last for several days. Maria continued to improve and became completely well. This assured the Indians we were not there to kill them as the *Senora* had said.

A few days later, the *Senora* and her son, Herman, took a load of skins, cassava roots, dried meat, and bananas to Iquitos. This was produce the Indians had brought her.

"Now that the *Senora* is in Iquitos, I think we should make the move to Miranyo," I suggested to Ruth.

For five *soles* a day I could get all the help I needed for the move. I asked a man named Enrique, who lived a half hour up the Napo, if he would round up several men to help me move. This is the same Enrique who put the floor in our house.

"No problem," he said.

The next morning Enrique showed up with five other men. We tied another canoe onto my big canoe and began loading our things into both canoes. Ruth was getting very good at packing on short notice.

With an empty canoe, I could make the trip to Miranyo in about two hours. With a loaded canoe and another tied alongside, it took from three to four hours to make the trip. The old 1928 Johnson was working well.

The move took several days, making two trips a day. In a letter Ruth wrote to her parents, she said:

As of 2:30 p.m. yesterday, Miranyo became our "home," so we're living out of boxes and duffel bags again. Bob is finally getting our things up here. On one load he was so heavily loaded, the canoe almost got swamped when he hit an unusually strong current. Poor fellow—he doesn't sunburn, but from being on the river so much lately his lips are parched and just won't heal. I've certainly been thankful I didn't have to make all those trips in the hot sun and then the cold rain.

Up until a week before we began to move, the river was so low he had to hunt for a pathway through all the sandbars which made it almost impassable. Just before Christmas it began to rain and the river came up at least 10 feet. It is going down now but isn't too bad yet. In a couple more days he ought to have all the materials from the house moved up here, so it has worked out just fine. But you can't imagine how tired we get of this moving around. Sometimes I'd give almost anything for a nice quiet hole to crawl into and just not come out for a long time....

It is now 2:45 p.m. and Bob just came with another load. He says the river is rising again so he can make the last two trips a lot easier. He's soaking wet and it's been raining all day. We got here yesterday just soaked, and I haven't had a chance to get the clothes washed and dried yet....

One of our chickens is determined to lay. She laid one egg in the basket on the way up here and laid another this morning....

Since all the materials were now at Miranyo and stored under Mr. Flores' house, we were ready to begin reconstruction. We were told the house would be reconstructed within a couple of weeks. However it took a little longer. Mr. Flores needed to leave for a few days and didn't want any construction while he was gone. When he returned he had Anacleto (Orejon man) and his family with him.

Anacleto was quite elderly. From each ear lobe hung large wooden ear disks about seven inches in diameter, made from the lightweight balsa tree. They were made white from a white clay. In the center was a small black circle made from a palm nut. His long, graying hair hung down to his shoulders, partly covering his bronzed, wrinkled face.

Also with him were his daughter and her two little girls, a small boy, and his son, Abelino. Abelino was very thin. By his cough and the lesion on his neck, we surmised he had tuberculosis.

By radio we talked with our doctor and told him of the symptoms. He concurred, it was probably tuberculosis. He said he would send medicine on our next service flight.

When the medicines arrived, we began administering them to Abelino with strict instructions. He was not to do any work, but to rest in his hammock, and that if he worked, he would die.

Mr. Flores didn't provide food for Anacleto and his family. They were expected to provide their own. This meant they didn't have much meat if any. With my rifle, I went into the jungle to shoot whatever bird I could find. Even if I found some that were not considered edible, they would be protein.

I brought the birds back to Anacleto to have him make soup for Abelino. I was trying to show him that Abelino needed meat, not just cassava roots and bananas, and that he could also catch fish for Abelino.

We explained to Mr. Flores that we would be going back to Yarina Cocha for a rest, and that Anacleto needed to care for Abelino until we could get back. He agreed.

I began working with Anacleto on the language but discovered a problem. He stuttered.

In another letter Ruth wrote her family:

> The informant the *patron* has given Bob is very willing, but he stutters. We don't know just how much Bob can do with him, but we're still trusting that the Lord will give us Miguel and Maria for teachers. The woman I have for an informant (Anacleto's daughter) lisps; she has a little twist I haven't heard before. We may turn up with an interesting version of this language with stuttering and lisping informants.

"Why don't we go to the village and see if Miguel and Maria would be willing to go to the base with us? There we would be able to work on the language uninterrupted," Ruth suggested. That sounded like a very good suggestion.

All the Indians, including those working for Mr. Flores, were dependent on their *patrons* for clothing. Originally, before the foreigners came, they went without clothing. Their blankets were made from pounded bark. If they were going to become a part of modern civilization, they needed a means of making their own clothing.

A friend in our church in Seattle worked for a sewing machine company, so we wrote and asked if he could locate two good Singer treadle machines. He wrote back that he already had two and was shipping them to us.

Before leaving to go back to Yarina Cocha, we made one last trip up the Sucusari to see if Miguel and Maria would come with us. All the Indians living on the Sucusari were gathered at Miguel's house: Luis (the chief) and his wife Nieves; their young son, Tito and daughter, Nancy; Gustavo and his wife, Sarah, and their children; Miguel and Maria; Daniel and Isidora, and their two children, Mateo and Irisi, and Hilario.

As I stepped into their house, I knew something was wrong.

"Why is everyone gathered here?" I asked Miguel.

"Before the *Senora* went to Iquitos, she told us that if we didn't work for her, we would have to move away because she owns all this land."

I knew this was not true because it is illegal to own the land on which the Indians are living. I had been told by Mr. Flores that *Senora* Rios doesn't even own the land on which her house is sitting—it belongs to the government.

"Miguel, that is not true. She does not own this land. Would you and Maria go with us to Yarina Cocha? I want you to talk with our director. He will help us get a letter from the Governor stating that this is your land."

"We will go with you. You have been nice to us. We want to build a house for you so you can live here," Miguel said.

"We would like that," I told them all. "We want to live here."

We returned to Miranyo with Miguel and Maria. The next morning the plane taxied up to our bank. Before we left, however, we gave strict instructions for Abelino to take the medicine every day, and for Anacleto to provide soup made from meat or fish. Further, Abelino was not to do any work; he was to rest every day.

Miguel and Maria had never flown in an airplane before. Naturally, both were very tense and scared. Before long both were very air sick and glad when they stepped out of the plane onto solid ground. They were immediately introduced to a completely different culture—a culture of indoor running water, telephones, indoor plumbing, wooden floors, and walls. They had just stepped from a stone-age culture into one somewhat modern.

Miguel and Maria were assigned to one of the several small houses constructed on our base for Indians brought to work with translators. The houses are small but adequate. They both seemed happy to have a place of their own because they knew they would be here for an extended period of time. They didn't know when we would be returning them to their village. They didn't seem worried, though, because they were being treated well. They liked having plenty to eat without having to hunt for it. Many of the families living on the base invited them to their homes and served cake and ice cream. They really enjoyed that.

Finally, we were able to work on the language without interruptions.

Yarina Cocha (Palm Lake)

One of the base houses at Yarina Cocha

The Secoya's chief's wife on the left. Notice the designs painted on their bodies.

Two Secoya Indian boys

One of our many jungle houses. This is the one we brought by canoe to Miranyo.

Heysoos, an Orejon Indian from the Amazon jungle of Peru

Chief Luis of the Orejones

Orejon man

The Sucusari when it is low. This is when Miguel told us we
were their prisoners because we couldn't get out.

Luis is admiring Nancy's new dress which Nieves sewed after
Ruth taught her to sew

The elephant Mateo wanted me to carve

Wild pig skins drying in the sun.
The large communal house is in the background.

Ruth teaching Nieves to cut a dress using a pattern

Tito, the boy killed by an electric eel

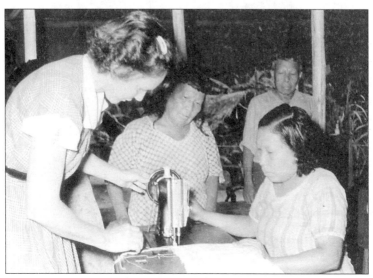

Ruth teaching Isidora to sew.
Her parents, Miguel and Maria, looking on.

Our jungle home on the Sucusari

9 | From Slavery to Freedom

AFTER ONE OF THE SUNDAY MORNING SERVICES, WE were asked to give a report on our time in the tribe. While others told of the great successes they were having in language study, all we could report were the difficulties we were having just getting into the tribe. Not a very glowing report.

Later in the week our director asked us to stop by his office. "When you go back with Miguel and Maria, I don't think Ruth should go. Instead, I'll send Gene Scott with you because I imagine you will be making several trips to Iquitos to talk with the Governor of the area," Mr. Townsend suggested.

"If we're going to be able to work with the people, we are going to have to obtain a letter or something indicating the Indians are not slaves to the *Senora*," I said. "Where we are now is not a very good language situation. Besides, we get interrupted so often to repair outboard motors and to treat the sick living along the Napo. The nearest medical facilities are in Iquitos, a long and difficult trip, so we end up treating them. We are happy to be of service, but that isn't why we are there."

Miguel and Maria seemed to enjoy their stay at Yarina Cocha, but after a month they were getting anxious to go home. Maria was worried about her daughter and grandchildren. She also missed her animals. She loved animals. Their house was always alive with parakeets, parrots, macaws, toucans, and a variety of wild four-legged creatures. The Secoyas didn't have dogs, but the Orejones had several they used for hunting deer and wild pigs.

During this time at Yarina Cocha, the sewing machines arrived. I showed Miguel and Maria the sewing machines and said, "Here are the sewing machines we promised you. We will be taking these with us when we go back."

A broad smile spread across his round face. His dark eyes darted from one machine to the other. "Now we won't have to depend on the *Senora* to make clothes for us."

Maria smiled and said, *"Dea."* They don't have a single word for wonderful, or very good. *"Dea"* serves for all of them.

We were making good progress on the language, but we knew we couldn't keep Miguel and Maria forever at the base. We had to make plans to return them.

Gene stopped by. "Uncle Cam tells me I am to go with you in place of Ruth."

"Are you free to do so?" I asked.

"Sure, whenever you are ready, I'll be ready," Gene said.

"All you will need is your sleeping bag, mosquito net, and, if you have a camera, take it along. Ours was stolen, so we don't have one."

A few days later, Gene, Miguel, Maria, and I were winging our way back to our house at Miranyo. With a good tail wind, we made it to Iquitos in record time—two and a half hours. This time, Miguel and Maria were veteran travelers and enjoyed the flight.

As soon as we landed in Iquitos, I went to the Governor's office. Our meeting was very cordial, and he assured me he, too, wanted all the Indians free.

"If there is anything I can do for you, I am at your service," he said.

It was too late for the pilot to take us to Miranyo and still be able to get back to Yarina Cocha the same day, so we spent the night in Iquitos, giving us time to do a little shopping.

We booked rooms in one of the two hotels in Iquitos—on the second floor. It only had two floors. Maria was reluctant to sleep that high off the ground. She was sure the building would fall down in the night. After much coaxing, we assured her she was safe.

Early the next morning we left for Miranyo. The river was too high for us to land in front of our house so the pilot landed a short distance upriver.

When the river is at its normal height there is a shelf that protrudes into the river providing a natural dock. From there, it is a steep climb up the slippery bank to the trail that leads to our house. When the river is high, there is no place for the plane to tie up, so we had to find another docking spot a short distance upriver.

From where the plane docked, we didn't know how we would get from there to our house because there is a wide *quebrada* (river) that flows from a lake, and no bridge.

However, before we left for Yarina, I had asked a Peruvian friend, who lives across the Napo, to keep my canoe for me. When we arrived, to our astonishment, my canoe was tied in front of where we landed.

Our house was in pretty good shape. Maria immediately began sweeping out the bat droppings and tidying up. That evening, I began eliminating some of the bats with my .22 rifle. Grass had grown high around the house, but with his machete, Miguel made short work of that. Soon the house was livable again, and after a meal of rice and canned tuna, I walked over to the Indians' house to inquire about Abelino. He was not in his hammock. In fact, his hammock was no longer where it had been.

"Where is Abelino?" I asked.

With sadness in his voice, Anacleto said, "Abelina was cured, so he and I paddled up the Sucusari. When we arrived at the village, he vomited up blood and died."

"I told him not to work. Because he did, he is now dead," I reminded them all. For Abelino, the Bible did not get translated in time.

Maybe I wasn't specific enough. Possibly, to them, paddling a canoe was not considered work. Whatever the reason, he felt strong enough to make the trip, and not knowing the damage tuberculosis does to the lungs, he died. We were very sorry to lose him.

It was too late in the day for us to make the trip to the village up the Sucusari, so we decided to wait until the next day. Besides, I needed to check in with the *patron* to let him know we were back.

I wrote in my journal:

> It must have been the fifth that we returned Miguel and Maria to the village. Just before we got to the mouth of the Sucusari, we saw two canoes take off from the

Senora's. Isidora and Sarah recognized my canoe and came to meet us. All of them embraced as soon as our canoes stopped side-by-side. They told us that Aurora, the *Senora's* daughter-in-law, was the only person in the house, and she was very sick. They also told us several of the Indians were in Iquitos with the *Senora*.

We stopped at the *Senora's* house so I could check on Aurora to see if there was anything I could do for her. She appeared to have a very bad cold and headache. I gave her several aspirins, talked with her for a while and then left for the village. Darkness descended upon us about half way up the Sucusari, so we had to go the rest of the way by flashlight. By the time we finally arrived, the flashlight batteries were almost exhausted. At one point we became stuck on a submerged log. Isidora offered to dive under the canoe and lift it up while we all paddled to get it off the log. It took her several dives, though, before we finally got free.

"Where is everyone?" I asked as we entered the big communal house.

"The *Senora* has taken Hoya, Hilario, Gustavo, and Francisco up the Nanay River to cut rosewood."

"Did they want to go?" I asked, being pretty sure they didn't.

"No, they didn't want to go, but the *Senora* made them."

"Would you go and get them back?" Miguel asked.

"I don't know, Miguel. I will talk with the Governor."

The next morning, Gene and I were getting ready to go to Iquitos to talk with the Governor. Then we heard the sound of a motor in the distance. Soon a canoe rounded the bend just below the village and into the bank. Herman, the

Senora's son, walked up to the house. Hoya was right behind him.

As Herman climbed the notched pole, I could feel the tension mounting. "Where are Gustavo, Hilario, and Francisco?" I asked.

"They are working for me up the Nanay River," he answered in a rather defiant tone.

"When are you going to bring them back? Miguel tells me you took them even though they didn't want to go," I questioned.

"They will come back when we bring them back," he said with a sneer.

"Does Hoya want to go with you?" I asked.

"He goes when I tell him," he responded with a finality in his voice that told me to quit asking questions.

I turned to Hoya and asked, "Do you want to go with Herman?"

His short answer was, "No."

In the best Spanish I could muster, I spelled out for Herman the rights of the Indians.

"These people are not your slaves," I told him. He quickly walked down the steps to his canoe, turned it around and left—without Hoya.

Before going to Iquitos, we needed to go to Miranyo to pack for an extended stay in Iquitos.

We arrived at Miranyo later that day and spent the night. Early the next morning we began to pack, but we also needed to return to the village to pick up Hoya. We wanted him with us when we talked with the Governor. We also needed him if we were going to go and get the others because he knew where we could find them.

When we arrived at the village, Hoya was ready to

accompany us. As we left, Miguel shouted, "Bring back Irisi; the *Senora* has her in Iquitos. And bring back my shotgun Herman took out of my house when we were gone to Yarina Cocha."

The Sucusari was full of water and we drifted rapidly down the river. Several caiman splashed into the river as we approached them. Colorful parrots and macaws flew overhead and monkeys rustled the tree tops. I always enjoyed the trips when we just drifted down the river. When we used the noisy outboard, we seldom saw wildlife.

We told Miguel we would bring a policeman back with us to assure them they were no longer slaves. We also told them we would return in a few days, but those few days stretched into two weeks.

Traveling turned out to be slower than usual once we got to the Napo River. The old Johnson broke down and we had to use the 2 h.p. Swedish Penta, which Ruth had likened to an egg beater.

We spent the night near the mouth of the Napo because we knew we couldn't make it all the way to Iquitos in one day with the little Penta.

Early the next morning we reloaded the canoe and were ready to leave. Because the canoe was loaded in the middle with all our gear, we had to walk along the gunwale of the canoe to get from the front to the back. It was my turn to operate the motor so I began gingerly walking along the gunwale of the canoe. To have the camera accessible, one of us had placed it on the seat next to the motor. As I stepped on the gunwale, the canoe tipped, dumping me and the camera into the river.

"Oh no!" I called out.

"What's wrong?" Gene asked.

"I just dumped your camera into the river."

"That wasn't my camera," Gene said as he walked over to the canoe. "I borrowed it from Mrs. Cudney."

"Oh no!"

Gene took off his clothes and dove several times into the river trying to locate the camera, but he came up empty-handed.

"Gene, you dive again and I'll pray," I suggested. He dove once more and came up with the camera. He kidded me for a long time about his having to do all the diving while I stayed in the canoe to pray. He just didn't know how hard I prayed.

Gene opened up the camera to let the sun dry it. After it appeared to be dry, he tried it—and it worked!

Because of the camera problem we didn't leave until about 9:00 a.m., and as we were using the small motor, we didn't make it to Iquitos that day. We had to spend another night on the mosquito-infested Amazon. We left early the next morning, but about half-way to Iquitos, a tropical storm pounded us, making travel very slow. We finally arrived about noon, cold and hungry. At the inlet that served as a makeshift port, we hired a family living on a house-raft to guard our canoe. We made our way up the slippery slope leading to town and checked into the hotel Iquitos. After a change of clothing, we headed for town.

As we were walking along main street, the governor drove by and spotted us. "Are you in town doing your shopping?" he asked.

"No, we are here to talk with you. We have a little problem."

"Hop in, I'm on my way to my office now." The three of us piled into his car for the short drive to his office.

As we stepped into his office, he settled back in his chair behind his desk and asked, "Now, what is your problem?"

"Some of the Orejones have been taken up the Nanay River to work, against their will. With your permission, *Senor* Governor, we would like to get them back home. *Senor* Governor, this is Hoya. He is an Orejon and knows where they are."

The governor shook Hoya's hand and asked, " Do you speak Spanish?" I answered for him and said he understood a little Spanish.

The governor picked up the phone and dialed the commander of the police. "I am sending two of my friends to see you. Take care of them," he said in a very authoritative voice. We thanked him and left his office.

As we entered the commander's office, he extended his hand and asked what he could do for us.

"Several Orejon men have been taken up the Nanay River to work rosewood against their will. Their families at the village would like to have them brought back. Also, *Senora* Rios has Irisi here in Iquitos against her will. The Indians want her returned to her family."

The commander immediately .issued an order to put two uniformed police at our disposal to accompany us up the Nanay River, and another order for a policeman to pick up Irisi, and yet another order for two policemen to accompany us back to the village up the Sucusari when we had the Indians.

Everything began to happen so fast. We weren't all that ready, but we realized what was happening was out of our hands. Just then an army captain walked in and recognized me. We had met about a year before. He came over and gave me a real *brazo* (embrace). He told the police captain, "Take good care of my friend."

A short time later, another policeman came in escorting the *Senora* and Irisi. Without telling the *Senora* to sit down he asked, "Are you the owner of the Orejones?"

"Yes, I am," she replied.

In a very stern voice the captain asked again, "Are you the owner of the Orejones?"

Realizing what she had said, she replied, "No, they work for me."

The captain then got rather rough with her and told her in very plain Spanish, "In this day and age, people do not own people...." He gave her a lengthy lecture. When he was through, she must have felt about 5 inches high. She always walked with a slouch, but when she left the office, the slouch was even more pronounced.

When the *Senora* was out of hearing range, the captain said, "I have two policemen to accompany you up the Nanay. When do you want them?"

We weren't ready for such quick action. We really didn't want Irisi in our custody; we just wanted her returned to her family. About the only thing we could do was take Irisi to a missionary's house and pawn her off on their daughter. Esther kindly agreed to keep Irisi until we could get her back with her family.

The captain told us to be at his office at eight in the morning, ready to go up the Nanay to bring back the Indians. We arose early and began getting everything we needed loaded into the canoe. By 8:00 a.m. we were at his office.

Hoya said it would take three days—two up and one back. That became a standing joke.

We left Iquitos at 9:15 a.m. I was surprised at the sparseness of houses along the Nanay. We did not come upon any houses until 5:00 p.m. We spent the night there and the next day, one of the policemen asked if we could go to the Civil Guard Post at a place called Santa Maria (that seemed to be a popular name for settlements), because he was out of cigarettes. Santa Maria was farther than we had expected. We didn't arrive until 8:00 p.m.

The unseen hand of God was again directing because the policeman at the Civil Guard Post knew approximately where *Don* Benigno and the Indians were working and gave us "good" directions.

We were told we could save a lot of time by taking a shortcut. "Take a left about two bends up the river. You will have to go through some brush, but you will come out further up river, because the river makes a big bend and almost meets itself there," we were told.

The question is, "How far is two bends?" When the river is squiggly, how can you tell which ones are the two bends? We could only guess.

After about fifteen minutes of pulling the canoe through a swamp blocked by brush and logs, we finally came out the other side. Whoopee! We had made a complete circle and ended up downriver instead of upriver. After a good laugh, we decided we'd better stick to the Nanay and not try anymore shortcuts.

About 11:30 a.m. the next day, Hoya pointed to the bank and shouted something in Orejon. We turned the canoe around and headed for the bank. A very large anaconda (nearly 20 feet long) was fighting with a 5-foot caiman. The snake was winning. The two were thrashing around in the shallow water, but the more the caiman fought, the tighter the snake squeezed until it broke the caiman's back. We watched the fight for about thirty minutes, then we decided we needed to be on our way. Besides, I didn't have my movie camera with me. In fact, we didn't have a camera because the one we borrowed quit working after its bath in the Napo River.

By believing Hoya, we only brought food for about four days. We were getting low. I had my shotgun, but we didn't see anything to shoot.

We were now on our fourth day out. At 5:00 p.m. we pulled into another settlement—that of a *patron* and several families of Iquitos Indians. We didn't know there were any pure Iquitos Indians still living. I was able to get a word list from them to send back to Yarina Cocha.

One of the ladies fixed us a nice dinner and I was able to purchase a smoked *sajino* (pronounced sahino) leg (another type wild pig), cassava roots, and bananas. We had planned on spending the night, but just then a larger river boat came by on its way up the Nanay to purchase rosewood.

The captain looked at our canoe and could see we were loaded for traveling and asked, "Where are you going?"

"We are looking for some Orejones who have been taken away to work without their consent," we said.

"I am going upriver to buy rosewood. Would you like to come along? You will make better time because I will be traveling most of the night."

We tied the canoe on behind and climbed in. We left San Antonio (many of the towns are named after Saints) about 6:00 p.m. and traveled until about midnight at which time he pulled to shore and tied up.

"We will spend the night here and leave first thing in the morning," the captain informed us.

We made soup from the *sajino* leg and cassava roots,

118

then tried to find a place to lie down so we could get some sleep. We didn't sleep very much that night. The mosquitoes were having a real banquet.

The captain let a very intoxicated man get on board. Pedro, in his drunken stupor, was very boisterous—just plain obnoxious. He talked or sang most of the night as he sipped from his bottle.

We left about 6:00 a.m. and shortly arrived at a *tambito* where Hoya said the four of them and *Don* Benigno slept on their first night.

"Are you looking for three Indians and a Peruvian? I know where they are. They are working up that little river." Pedro pointed to a small stream that flowed into the Nanay.

I asked the captain how much I owed him and he said, "100 *soles*." That seemed like an exorbitant price, but since the policemen were with me, I didn't argue. I just paid him. When I told the police how much he charged, they commented, "I would have said thank you and left."

The launch did, however, save us two days traveling plus the gasoline it would have taken.

Gene and I thought we had given Satan an advantage by listening to a drunk, but Hoya assured us, they were indeed inland, and he could find them.

"Do you know of any other Indians who are working rosewood in the area?" we asked Pedro. He was quite sober by now since he had emptied his bottle during the night.

"Yes, about two hours by outboard there is another man cutting rosewood.

We decided to go the two hours to see if *Don* Benigno might be there. About five bends (by our estimate of a bend) we encountered the launch we had ridden. The Captain had stopped and was talking with two men in a canoe; they were pointing downstream. As we neared them, we asked if they had seen three Indian men and a Peruvian.

"As we came by yesterday, there were three Indian men and a Peruvian camped at the *tambito* just below. Above the *tambito* is a small river—they are working up that river. It is too small for your motor, but you can paddle up it for quite a ways," they said.

Hoya had been right, but we weren't sure because it had been several days since Herman had taken Hoya with him back to the village.

We returned to the small river and decided to paddle. An hour later we came to their camp, but the only ones there were a woman we didn't know and her two small children—the wife and children of a Peruvian working with *Don* Benigno.

Gene looked around and commented, "I wonder what *Don* Benigno is planning on feeding these people?"

"I don't know. There doesn't seem to be any food around here that I can see," I said. "There aren't any stores for miles."

Gene and I decided to go with Hoya to find Hilario, Gustavo, and Francisco. We didn't want them to see the policemen for fear they would run. The *Senora* had instilled fear in the people that she would have the police put them in jail if they didn't work for her.

We hadn't walked more than about ten minutes when we came upon Gustavo and Francisco. They were glad to see us and their first words were, "We don't want to work rosewood."

Except for Hilario, we could have left, but we didn't want to leave without him. The Peruvians had taken Hilario with them to look for more rosewood trees. Gustavo didn't know where they were nor how long they would be gone, but we decided to stay a while and wait. It was beginning to rain, so the two of them constructed a small shelter from palm fronds.

Around 4:00 p.m. Pedro came looking for us. He took my machete and said he was going to go look for Hilario. The rain had stopped, so we decided to go with him. He seemed to know that area pretty well.

After about a thirty-minute walk, we found another *tambito*. Since it was beginning to rain again, we decided to stay there for a while. It was still raining when Hilario showed up. He was somewhat startled to see us, but his first words were also, "I don't want to work rosewood. I want to go home."

We all walked back to the canoe. When the three of them saw the policemen in their uniforms, we could see they were somewhat disturbed.

"These policemen have come with me to take you back home," I reassured them.

Although it was getting late, we decided to leave anyway and go as far as the *tambito* at the mouth of the little river. Pedro decided to stay.

When we got to the *tambito*, I looked for my machete. It was gone along with Pedro. It must have stuck to his hand.

We left the next morning at the first sign of daylight. The trip was rather uneventful and we made it to San Antonio by noon where the *patron's* wife cooked us another very nice meal of boiled wild pig and cassava root. I was also able to get a longer word list from one of the Iquitos Indians. We learned there were more Iquitos Indians living up another river called the Chambira. We decided not to look for them at this time, but to come back later to conduct a more thorough survey.

We arrived at Santa Maria around 5 o'clock that afternoon and were able to purchase more food: a chicken, cassava roots, and rice. There were now eight of us in the canoe and eight large men can consume a lot of food. We spent the night at Santa Maria and left the next morning for Iquitos.

The slow-moving Nanay is more like a lake than a river. It didn't flow very fast, so the 2 h.p. Penta couldn't make very good time. We had expected to arrive in Iquitos the next day. When we stopped for the night, the chicken, cassava roots, and rice didn't go very far, but we did save a little for breakfast the next morning.

After a very meager breakfast, we started off on the last leg of what was supposed to be our four-day journey. We had already been gone seven days. We were all getting pretty hungry when one of the men spotted a large bird in the top of a tree. I didn't think my shotgun would carry that far, but I took careful aim, pulled the trigger, and the bird fell to the ground with a thud.

I turned the canoe around and headed for shore. One of the men went looking for the bird and came back with it. We cleaned the bird and made soup. It wasn't much for eight of us, but we shared. At least it took the edge off our hunger.

Later the same afternoon we pulled into the harbor below Iquitos. As soon as we tied up the canoe, we headed for our favorite restaurant and had their *Plato Atomico*, a large mound of rice in the center of the plate topped with slices of pork, beef, or chicken, cut up vegetables, and crowned with a sunny-side-up fried egg. The Indians had never eaten in a restaurant before, so having to use a knife and fork was a new experience. Eating from a table was also new for them. Their custom is for everyone to sit cross-legged in a circle around a large pot of boiled meat, cassava roots, and plantains served on banana leaves.

We enjoyed the company of the two policemen and they seemed to have enjoyed going with us. We said good-bye to them and the six of us checked into the cheaper of the two hotels in town.

We had lost track of the days and didn't realize it was Sunday until I saw the date on a newspaper. I suggested to Gene we take the three men to Esther's and check on Irisi.

The church that was started by Esther's parents was right next door to their house. When we got there, church service was already in progress so we all took a seat in the back. I am not sure the Indians understood much of what was said, but they all sat quietly throughout the entire service.

After the service, Irisi rushed back to greet us, especially Hilario, Gustavo, and Francisco. She was surprised to see them.

"Irisi likes cake and ice cream," Esther said with a twinkle in her eye. "We had a good time together even though I don't speak her language and she doesn't understand much Spanish."

Irisi had on a pretty dress that Esther had made her. "The only dress she had when she arrived was a well-worn, badly stained dress, so I made her this one," Esther continued. "She seems really pleased."

"After you get settled in the hotel, come back and I will prepare supper for you," Esther said. She prepared a wonderful meal for us—including cake and ice cream. The three men had never eaten cake and ice cream before.

"Do you like it?" I asked.

"*Dea*," they all replied. "*Frio*" (cold) they said as they ate the ice cream.

10 | The *Senora* and Her Daughter

AS WE WERE MAKING PLANS TO RETURN HOYA, Hilario, Gustavo, Francisco, and Irisi to their families at the village, I had Gene bring the big canoe around to the other side of Iquitos and park it in the cove just below the Peru Hotel so we wouldn't have to go so far to load it. Meanwhile, I took the Indians to Esther's house to wait with Irisi until we were ready to go. I left them there, so I could return to the hotel to pack our things, and to do some needed shopping.

Now that I was alone, I could get the buying done quicker and we could be on our way.

As I stepped out of the hotel, whom should I run into but the *Senora's* daughter, another woman, and Isidora, Irisi's mother.

While we were up the Nanay bringing back the men, Herman had gone to the village and told the people I had taken Irisi and had her put in jail, and that she was dying. We now knew the club the *Senora* was holding over their heads—the fear of incarceration and death at the hands of the police and the military.

Isidora was very angry with me for treating her daughter like that. Her first words were, "What are you doing, and where is Irisi?"

Next, the *Senora's* daughter started in on me. Her mouth was as vile as her mother's. She called me every name under the Peruvian sun. "Where is Irisi? Isidora wants her back now!"

"Fine," I said. "Follow me." Esther's house was only about a block away, so we walked to her house. The daughter kept ranting and raving the entire distance.

They weren't expecting such a turn of events. As Esther opened the door, there stood Hoya, Gustavo, Francisco, Hilario, and Irisi. The daughter was speechless. She didn't know we had gone up the Nanay to bring the men back. Irisi's mother seemed completely confused. Here was her daughter in a pretty new dress not crying at all. They all just stood there, not knowing what to do.

"Gustavo, come with me to talk with my mother," the *Senora's* daughter ordered.

"I don't want to," Gustavo replied.

"Francisco, you come with me to talk with my mother."

"I don't want to," was his answer.

"She wants to talk to you."

"I don't want to," he again replied.

"Hilario, let's go talk to my mother."

"I don't want to," was his reply.

Then the daughter turned to me and said, "You have them well trained in what to answer, don't you?"

Then she said, "My mother wants to talk with you and solve this problem without the authorities." I was suspicious.

I tried to explain, once again, that I was not interested in going into business—I didn't want to be a *patron.* All I wanted to do was assure the Indians they were free and not slaves to anyone. We just wanted to live among them and learn their language.

The *Senora's* daughter was becoming more and more belligerent and abusive. She insisted I accompany her to talk with her mother. I finally consented, just to get her out of Esther's house. I had no intention of going to see her mother, because I knew I would not come out alive—I would end up in the bottom of the Amazon River. On at least two occasions, the *Senora* had given shotgun shells to the Indians to kill me.

As we left the house and were walking, I suggested we all go to the governor's office and talk with him.

"He is not in his office," the *Senora's* daughter said.

"It doesn't matter because we have to make an appointment anyway," I suggested.

"My mother is too sick to go that far."

I was sure then, they wanted me behind closed doors, and I wasn't about to let myself get put in that position.

We caught the bus that took us to her house, and as we stepped off the bus, the daughter grabbed my arm and said, "It will only take five minutes to resolve the problem."

I started walking toward the governor's office. Since Alicia (the daughter) couldn't get me into her house, she decided to go with me. Just then, *Don* Benigno stuck his head out the door and asked, "Where are you going?"

"We are going to the governor's office. Want to come along?"

"I have other engagements," he said.

All we really did was take up the governor's time. I didn't

make any accusations against the *Senora*, *Don* Benigno, Herman, nor the daughter. The daughter didn't say anything. I just told the Governor we wanted to stop by to visit (which I had done several times before).

After we left his office, the daughter felt she had gained a victory and began taunting me with, "What are you going to do, feed the Indians canned foods and give them new clothing? With you they will have everything they want without working."

I let her rant on, then excused myself. I did go back to the governor's office to apologize for taking up his time. Before I left, I asked him what his wishes were in the matter of the *Senora*.

"Keep on doing what you are doing, everything is fine," he assured me.

Next, I went to the police captain's office.

"Have you returned Irisi to her mother?" he asked.

"Yes, I have."

"Good, the *Senora* was in my office accusing you of taking Irisi for immoral purposes. She wanted to know why I would allow two *Gringos* to take Irisi. But I understand you left her at the missionary's house."

"We did, and now she is with her mother," I told him. "I have come back for the purpose of having a policeman accompany me to the village to tell the Indians they are free."

At the mouth of the Napo River was another Civil Guard Post called Orellana, named after the first Spaniard to discover the Napo River. The captain inserted a sheet of paper into his typewriter and typed an order for two policemen from Orellana to accompany me to the village.

It was now May 23 and we were finishing up our purchases. However, we were wondering how we were going to get the items purchased (including two 15-gallon drums of gasoline and a drum of kerosene), the Indians, and two policemen from Orellana, in the canoe. Just then, the Spaniard who had guarded my canoe and four chickens, and who did most of the work on our house at Miranyo spotted me.

"*Don* Roberto, so good to see you!" I still owed him some money for the work he did on the house. He continued, "I am without any money. Could you pay me a few *soles*? I am broke, and I need money to buy some things and get home."

"Of course." I then gave him 200 *soles*. "When are you going home?"

"I am leaving as soon as I buy a few things I need."

"Do you have room to take some of my things? I am too heavily loaded."

"I would be happy to take some of your things," he said.

This was a real answer to a pressing need. Mario was able to take Gustavo and Francisco plus my drums, leaving plenty of room for the two policemen.

We were only about forty-five minutes away from Iquitos when a storm hit. The river became very choppy; waves were beginning to splash into the canoe. We decided we had to stop and pulled to shore below a small house, a *tambito* that was erected for the people who tended the large garden.

We stayed there until about 4:00 p.m., then decided we had better return to Iquitos. The storm was so strong it took the little Penta three hours to make it back. Iquitos juts into the Amazon River restricting the flow of the tons of water that rushes past the town causing a very swift current. The little Penta just couldn't make any headway trying to push the heavily-loaded canoe, so everyone in the canoe began paddling. Slowly we inched our way forward. Finally, about 7:30 p.m. we made it to port. We were thoroughly drenched and very cold.

The port is made up of grass huts on a floating island of logs. I tied the canoe in front of one of the houses and paid the family to guard our things. Then we trudged up the slippery hill to the Peru Hotel—but there weren't any vacancies. We had only one alternative—go back to Esther's.

As Esther opened the door, she saw a wet, soggy-looking bunch. She apologized for laughing, "You people look terrible. Come on in."

"We are sorry to trouble you again, but the hotel is full."

"I'm glad you came. You are always welcome," she said with real assurance in her voice.

She told us to clean up while she prepared dinner. She is a wonderful cook and prepared a sumptuous meal for all of us. We all bedded down on the living room floor for the night. The next morning, May 24, Esther prepared fried eggs, toast, jam, and coffee. The Indians had never eaten a meal like that, but they ate it and when I asked them if they liked it, they all said, "*Dea.*"

It was still raining, but we decided we had to leave, rain or shine. However, when we finally shoved off, the rain cloud stayed behind us. We could see the rain following us, but it never did catch us. We were traveling the same speed as the rain cloud.

Rain in the tropics is different. As one flies over the jungle and looks out over the vast green carpet, rain clouds are dripping rain over different areas. There may be a clump of rain clouds to your right; another may be 50 miles ahead of you, constantly moving. Flying through rain clouds is like driving over a very bumpy road at high speed. However, in a minute or two, the plane emerges on the other side, and is again in bright sunshine with smooth flying. The rain clouds remind me of huge lawn sprinklers put there to keep the jungle green.

We arrived at Orellana, at the mouth of the Napo River, about 4:00 p.m. As I walked up to the guard post, I greeted the corporal in charge and handed him the order from the police captain.

I am not sure he could read, because he stared at it a long time.

"Are there two policemen available to accompany me to the Sucusari?" I asked.

"No, *Senor*, there are only two of us here at the moment. The others are away. They will be back June third—you can take two of them then."

Just then Herman pulled up to the guard post, but as soon as he saw me, he took off. Since we knew Herman would be home and would probably go to the village ahead of us to get whatever products he could take from the Indians, I decided to ask the corporal, "Could I take one of you with me now with the promise to return tomorrow?"

"I don't like to leave the post with only one person, but if you bring him back tomorrow, I will let him go with you," he answered rather reluctantly. However, he did have a direct order from his captain, so he was in a bit of a quandary. Should he obey the captain's order, or both stay at the guard post as he knew they were supposed to?

We left and made it to Miranyo rather late. Traveling after dark is a bit risky. After a heavy rain upriver, whole islands float down the river—chunks of the river bank that have sloughed off into the river. However, it was a moonlit night, and we could see fairly well.

When we arrived at Miranyo, I was sick. I went to bed and let Gene and the Indians unload the canoe. We didn't have any beds, so we all slept on the floor. The next morning, we all went to the village. The policeman told the people, in Spanish, that they were not slaves to anyone, and Miguel translated. Fortunately, most of the people, plus some from another river, were there to hear the message.

If the rain had not made us return to Iquitos and delayed us a day, we wouldn't have known Herman was at home, and probably would have gone without the policeman. Another indication an unseen hand was directing.

"Was Irisi in jail?" Miguel asked.

"No, she wasn't."

"That's what I told Daniel and Isidora, but they believed the *Senora,*" he said. "I knew she wasn't."

In Spanish, I said, "If any of you go with anyone against your will again, I am not going to go and bring you back." I said this to Miguel and told him to tell all the people. The policeman voiced his agreement.

After a meal of smoked wild pig and cassava root, we headed back to Orellana. On the way, we stopped and had a talk with Herman. I wanted him to realize the Government of Peru was behind us and wanted the Indians free. The policeman assured him of that. Herman was very subdued. I asked him for Miguel's shotgun and he gave it to me. If the policeman hadn't been there, I am not sure he would have.

After dropping off the policeman, we spent the night at Orellana, and the next morning we returned to the village.

We all went to the chief's house a short distance up the Sucusari where we had a meeting of the "General Assembly of the Orejones" with the chief presiding. It was a very impressive meeting. There were about twenty of the Ore-jones present.

What was accomplished? (l) Irisi was again with her family, (2) Gustavo, Hilario, Francisco, and Hoya were back home, (3) Miguel had his shotgun back, and (4) I had brought the policeman I had promised them.

They were now free and they knew it. Gene put it this way, "I have never seen so much packed into three weeks in my life, and so little of our doings, everything of the Lord's doing."

11 | Our Move to the Village

A FEW DAYS LATER, A PLANE BROUGHT RUTH AND returned Gene to Yarina Cocha.

At long last, we were free to go to the village any time we wanted. And we did. Ruth and I went to the village as frequently as the Sucusari would allow us. Although we were called upon to bandage wounds, treat eye infections, and a host of other illnesses, we were where we heard the language every day. And we were learning. Little by little we were beginning to understand more and more of their language. We would stay for several days before returning to Miranyo. However, as soon as the Peruvians knew we were back, we had visitors.

"Good afternoon, *Don* Roberto. I have come to visit," Enrique said as he approached the house. This was their standard greeting before they asked what they wanted. After a few minutes of small talk, I asked, "What can I do for you?"

"My daughter is very sick. Would you please come and cure her?" They never asked me to just come and look at the person, I was always asked to cure them.

"Of course," I responded. "Let's go right now." I grabbed the bag containing our medicines, and we headed for the river.

We tied Enrique's one-man canoe onto my big canoe and started downriver. It was only about twenty minutes to his house. As we approached, Eurifina was sitting up, watching us tie up the canoe. A dirty rag wrapped around her jaw.

Eurifina looked to be about eighteen, a slender girl. Her jet black hair hung in a tangled mass to her shoulders, tangled from lying down and rolling her head from side to side trying to ease the pain.

"Let me look at you," I said as I removed the rag. I could see her jaw was badly swollen. She was in terrible pain. The infection had affected her joints so she could hardly walk.

There was no question, a badly infected tooth had to come out. In my medicine kit I had a pair of forceps my dentist cousin had given me. Just like my blowtorch and soldering iron, I had no idea why I would take it along, as I knew nothing of dentistry. But it was free, so I added it to the rest of the things we were taking. It seems we took along a lot of things without knowing why.

"I will have to pull the tooth without Novocaine because I don't have any," I informed them.

"Do whatever you have to do," Enrique said.

I held the girl's head firmly with my left arm, and with my right hand, began wiggling the tooth back and forth. I pulled and twisted as long as she could stand it, then relaxed a minute or two. I worked on that poor girl's tooth for more than an hour before the tooth gave way and came out. Sweat was streaming down both our faces and off our chins, but the tooth came out. I gave the girl a shot of penicillin and enough sulfa tablets for several days. For our services, Enrique gave us a hen. We named it Blondie. We probably should have named it Extraction.

Two weeks later, I stopped at Enrique's to see how the girl was doing. She was down at the creek washing clothes and feeling fine.

Another day, the Spaniard's wife (from across the Napo) brought their young son to me. He had an infection on top of his head that made him look like a cone-head. I took his temperature—102°F.

"I will have to call our doctor," I told them. I cranked up the generator and called Yarina. "Yarina, this is Sucusari calling."

"Sucusari, this is Yarina, go ahead."

"I need to ask Doc a few questions." The doctor came to the radio and I asked him what to do.

"Take a sharp razor blade, shave off the hair around the infection, then make a quick, deep cut near the base. With your hypodermic needle, extract the pus, bandage it and shoot him with penicillin."

I shaved off the hair around the infection, washed it with alcohol, then Ruth held the boy's head firmly while I made a quick incision. Blood began to flow freely. The mother screamed and began crying. I guess she thought I was going to cut his head off. With gauze, I stanched the flow of blood and with the needle extracted at least 30 c.c.'s of matter. I bandaged his head and shot him with penicillin. I also gave him enough sulfa tablets for several days. For my services we were given another chicken. We named it Blondie II. It proved to be our best egg producer.

"If we are going to get any language study done, we are going to have to move to the village," I lamented one day.

We decided to make another trip to the village. As I nosed the canoe into the bank, several of the men were there to greet us. We could see they had been drinking. Miguel hadn't. "Where did you get the *aguardiente*?"

"Herman came up and took three pig skins and gave us five bottles of *aguardiente*. He says we still owe him five skins."

Although I was able to obtain their freedom, old habits take a long time to die. They did not, yet, have the courage to resist the demands of Herman or the *Senora*.

"When are you going to bring the sewing machines and teach Isidora to sew?" Miguel asked.

"As soon as you build us a house, we will bring the sewing machines," we said.

"We will build you a house right away," Miguel assured us. "Why don't you move into our house until we get yours built? You could live at that end. " He pointed to the east end of the large communal house. All nodded their heads in agreement.

"You mean we have to move again?" Ruth said with a sigh. "I hope this is our last because I am tired of moving."

As we were about to leave, another Orejon family we hadn't met walked into the village. They had to leave their canoe down river, because the river was very low and there were too many logs, so they parked their canoe and walked to the village. He was introduced to us as Meleano. We soon excused ourselves and started for the river. It was getting late.

"If you are going to get home today, I better go along and help you get through all the logs that are across the river," Meleano offered.

We were happy for the offer and with a lot of *Setiko* bark (the bark that gets slippery when put in water) we were able to slide the canoe over the logs. We had to paddle the rest of the way down the Sucusari.

As we headed up the Napo, Hishuco and Guirino Flores waved for us to stop. Their house was about halfway to Miranyo.

"Two weeks ago my wife fell and hasn't been able to get up. Would you cure her?" By now our reputation as miracle workers had spread. The "miracle" was the radio, the medical doctor on the other end, the antibiotics, and prayer.

After taking a look at her, I realized I had better call Yarina again and consult with Doc. We went the rest of the way home with the promise that we would talk with our doctor and be back in the morning.

The next morning we called Yarina. "What can I do for a woman probably in her thirties who fell two weeks ago. She has large infected sores all over her body, and she has a high fever."

"Give her penicillin shots for five days and see how she reacts. If she hasn't improved, call me again."

I went every day to give her a shot of penicillin, read to the family from the book of Mark, and to pray with them. Slowly she began to improve and the sores began to dry up. In a couple of weeks, she was up and around.

We informed our host, *Senor* Flores, we were moving to the village. He wasn't very pleased, because he had hoped we would convince all the people up the Sucusari to move to his place so they could work for him. We never suggested that, because we couldn't see that he was treating his workers much better than the other *patrons*.

This time we didn't have to move a complete house—just our belongings, which included the heavy refrigerator and heavy tool box. Ruth began packing again. She was getting good at it.

As soon as the rains hit, and the Sucusari rose, we began what we hoped would be our last move. When we finally did get everything moved, we had taken up about a fourth of the communal house—one entire end. But we were there! Now we could really get into the language.

The Sewing Machines Arrive

12

ONE DAY WHEN THE SUCUSARI WAS AT ITS LOWEST, Miguel commented, "You are prisoners now. You can't get out." He was joking, of course, but it was true. When the river was at its lowest, there was very little water in it and we were stranded. Much of the area between the village and the Napo was swamp land. There were no trails. But we didn't mind at all. We were glad to be living in the village where we heard the Orejon language spoken every day all day long.

I was interested to see how fast the river did rise. When the river was at its lowest, I fastened a long pole in the middle of the river. When the river rose and crested, I measured the distance. The river had risen 9 feet in four hours.

The Orejones weren't like the Secoyas in that they didn't bother our things. We could live a pretty normal life on "our" end of the house.

At Miranyo I made a rather crude bedstead, table, and chairs, because we couldn't seem to adjust to sleeping on the floor and sitting on up-turned canoes, or even sitting in rocking hammocks. Our bones were too stiff for sitting cross-legged on our haunches, and eating our meals (using only a spoon and fingers) off banana leaves placed on the floor. Besides, the men ate first and the women ate what the men left. Ruth and I liked to eat together. Our cultural differences showed again.

On our next service flight, we planned on having our foam rubber mattress and the sewing machines flown out. We also wanted some fresh vegetables, which we sorely missed.

For greens, though, we did have access to palm hearts that Ruth made into a salad—a very tasty lettuce substitute. She could even make mayonnaise from turtle eggs.

Life was moving along very well, and our new home was taking shape. It wasn't going to be very big, but adequate for the two of us. I screened off half the area for our living quarters to keep out the millions of insects that either bit or stung us, and to give us more privacy.

We felt sorry for Hilario. He was patiently working and waiting for the day he could have his own home and Irisi for his wife. He worked hard, carrying water from the river, sweeping up around the house, bringing in fresh meat for the family, even doing a lot of the cooking. Irisi didn't seem to pay much attention to him. Hilario reminded us of Jacob in Genesis chapter 29, verses 15 to 25: "...So Jacob served (Laban) seven years for Rachel and they seemed to him but a few days because of his love for her...."

We checked in with the base every morning to let them know our status. If they needed to talk with us, the radio operator would call "Sucusari," and we would answer. The radio was like the early-days telephone party lines. Everyone listened in. There were no secrets.

A newly married couple working in another tribe radioed in and asked for an appointment with the doctor. "Doctor, every morning, I don't feel very well," the wife complained. When the couple arrived back at the base, a large group had gathered to sing, "Rock-a-bye baby...." "How did you know?" the wife questioned.

More and more Orejones began moving into the village. With the newcomers, it didn't take long to complete our small house. When it was completed, we moved from the big open-air communal house to our little private mansion.

"Sucusari, this is Yarina. A flight is scheduled for your area on Friday. Do you need anything?"

"We need the two sewing machines and our foam mattress. We would also appreciate some fresh vegetables." We had to pay our share of the cost of the flight, so we didn't have the plane come any more often than we had to, but we were always glad when it did so we could get our mail, and a few of the things we were more accustomed to eating, such as fresh carrots. At the base, fresh vegetables were trucked in from the coast.

One time Ruth asked for some carrots. The person in charge of shipping, a single man, selected one very large carrot. His thought was that one large carrot would be better than several smaller ones, because there wouldn't be so much waste. Apparently, he was not a cook. Ruth almost cried when she saw that great big carrot. But we ate it, and it was better than no carrot.

When there were long periods of time that we didn't receive mail, we dictated letters over the radio to a family at the base, who would write the letters and send them home for us. On one occasion, we had been given a baby monkey. As I dictated the letter over the radio, I told about the baby monkey. Well, it came across as baby buggy. When my mother received the letter, she wrote back, "I just hope you don't have a baby in those awful jungles."

The plane came and brought us the sewing machines, the foam rubber mattress, and a few fresh vegetables. As always, when we needed to use the river, it rose as though we controlled a valve at the headwaters. Our "personal valve Operator" again opened the flood gates and the river rose so we could meet the plane.

As soon as the sewing machine was set up, all the men, women, and children gathered around to watch as Ruth put a piece of cloth in the machine and began to sew. They were all smiling broadly and chatting among themselves.

Ruth immediately began teaching the women to sew, starting with Isidora. Ruth would demonstrate, and then let Isidora try. Isidora would tense up, step on the treadle and the machine would run backwards breaking the thread. After many tries and lots of broken threads, she finally got the machine to run the right direction. It wasn't long until all the women could sew on the machines. Ruth cut out paper patterns for dresses, blouses, skirts, pants, and shirts for each of the families. The dress Nancy is wearing (in the photo) was sewn by her mother, after Ruth taught her to sew. Of course, all this time Ruth was learning new words and phrases.

As Ruth began teaching the women to sew, I worked with the men teaching them to read numbers. If they were going to be independent, they had to know how to count in Spanish. The Orejon numbering system only went to five.

"Why do you only count to five?" I asked Miguel.

"We don't need any more numbers. We can't carry more than five things at a time."

144

I pointed out, however, if they were going to buy and sell, they had to know how to count. He agreed.

Our little house became the communal center for the entire village. They even brought their own hammocks to hang on our porch. This was wonderful for language learning, but not very good for privacy.

Ruth wanted a place cleared for her garden and hired Demas to cut the brush just below our house. He hadn't worked very long when he came running to our house.

"A *shushupi* just bit me," he said as he showed us the two fang marks on his ankle. His ankle was already beginning to swell. We hoped someone would still be on the radio, so I cranked up the generator and radioed the base. We needed the doctor's services again.

13 | The Snake Bite

"YARINA COCHA, THIS IS SUCUSARI, DO YOU READ me?"

The radio operator came on with, "This is Yarina, what do you need?"

"I need to talk with the doctor. A boy just got bit by a *shushupi*." In a few minutes the doctor was on the radio.

"Do you have a refrigerator?" the doctor asked.

"Yes, we have a small 2 ½ cu. ft. refrigerator."

"Does it have ice trays?" the doctor wanted to know.

"Yes, it does," I replied.

"Keep ice on the wound for as long as you can to keep down the swelling. They don't usually die from the snake bite, but from the secondary infection caused by the swelling that cuts off the blood flow."

The refrigerator had two tiny ice trays about 6 inches long by 3 inches wide and ½ inch deep. It would make ice twice a day, no more, but that was enough for us to have cold drinks.

The Indians had never seen a refrigerator before. In fact, they had never seen ice before. When they killed an animal, we would buy meat from them. One day, we purchased a quarter of a wild pig. Two days later, Ruth was cooking fresh wild pig from the refrigerator.

"Where did you get the fresh meat?" one of the men asked.

"We bought it from Daniel two days ago."

"Isn't it rotten?"

"No, it isn't," we told him.

"Why isn't it rotten?" one of the men asked with a very puzzled look on his face.

By then several men had gathered to hear the discussion. We showed them the refrigerator and gave them each a cube of ice. They began tossing the ice cube from hand to hand, all the time laughing at that strange little cold object. I then showed them the tiny flame burning at the base of the refrigerator, and then had them put their hand inside the refrigerator. I am sure they were very puzzled how a burning flame could make things cold.

We had Demas sit on our porch so he would be close to the refrigerator. As the ice melted, Ruth went to the refrigerator to fill up another bag. The little refrigerator kept making ice until about five that afternoon when the swelling went down. Then a strange thing happened. The refrigerator quit making ice.

The next day, the refrigerator went back to making ice twice a day. It would not make any more.

Doc also told us to give him a series of penicillin shots. Although the swelling had gone down, there appeared a very nasty sore where the fangs penetrated the skin.

We kept treating Demas until, one day, we went to

148

change the bandage and found a greenish-gray mass plastered over the wound.

"What is that?" I asked.

"The witch doctor has started treating me."

"If you want the witch doctor to treat you, fine. But we won't continue with our treatment," I informed him.

A few days later, Demas was sitting in his house with a distraught look on his face. He looked as though he had lost his last friend.

"What's the matter?" I asked.

Without saying anything, he showed me his leg. The swelling was back, and the wound was all puffy and red.

"Do you want us to start treating you again?" He nodded his head.

"If we treat you, the witch doctor cannot. If he treats you, we will again stop."

"The witch doctor will not treat me," he answered.

The wonders of penicillin. The witch doctor thought he could take credit for Demas surviving a *shushupi* bite. Very few ever survived.

We started him on penicillin again, and before long, he was completely well.

The Peruvians told me of a great snake bite remedy. "Cut off about 6 inches of the snake's tail (you have to catch it first), swallow the tail and take a big swallow of kerosene. *Es un gran remedio, Senor*" (It's a great remedy). It really was, because the victims always died. They didn't have to worry about snakes anymore.

Life was really wonderful living among the Orejones. As they brought us wild meat, bananas, or cassava roots, we weighed each item and paid them according to the price on the Napo River. In this way, we were teaching them the use of money.

We hadn't seen the *Senora* or Herman for several weeks. Then one day, we heard the roar of an outboard motor coming up the river. It was Herman. He didn't stop where we were, but went on up river to the chief's house.

About an hour later, the chief walked in. "How much should I charge Herman for a basket of cassava roots?"

"They charge two *soles* on the Napo," I told him. He then left but came back a short time later.

"Herman wants a wild pig. How much should he pay?" I again told him what they pay on the Napo. He walked back to his house. Soon, Herman came by, headed downriver.

We were elated. Herman could no longer steal from them. He now had to pay for the things he took. They were finally realizing they were free at last.

"I made Herman dig his own cassava roots," the chief told us with a little twinkle in his eyes.

"*Dea,*" we replied.

The Indians' diet consists mainly of what the jungle provides: wild pigs, deer, anteaters, monkeys, fish, and a few other items like fat, juicy grubs from a palm tree. They grow bananas and cassava roots. There are also a few wild fruits they gather. One fruit called *pijuayo* (pronounced pihuayo) is placed in large earthenware pots, covered with water, and placed in the sun to ripen. When ripe, the women place the split *pijuayo* in a canoe-like trough and mash with a wooden pestle. As it turns into a mash, they chew blobs of it and spit it back into the mash. The saliva acts like brewer's yeast, and after a day or two, it ferments. If left for a week, it becomes very alcoholic—but it was more nutritious than *aguardiente*, the sugarcane liquor.

Although we ate well, we were not accustomed to a

steady diet of jungle foods, so we had flour, rice, salt, sugar, and some canned foods brought in.

We had been in the village for several weeks and were running short of our *Gringo* food supplies. We needed to go to Iquitos to replenish our larder with our kind of food, and to buy lumber for a desk and shelving. Our supply of kerosene was also getting low. By now, a few days' rest would be a relief, because we were on duty twenty-four hours a day. We needed some time to ourselves. The stress was getting to us.

14 | An Unforgettable Trip

WE TOLD THE INDIANS WE NEEDED TO GO TO IQUI-tos to buy kerosene, gasoline, lumber, and other things. Also that we would be going alone because there wouldn't be room for more bodies on the way back. (Besides, we wanted to be alone to have at least a few days to ourselves. Even when we went inside and shut the door, many would stand outside peering in watching our every move.)

One time, a pastor from Chicago was brought out to visit our village and get a feel of what missionary life was like. After several days, he complained, "Could you please have the people quit standing around watching us all the time?"

"You came to look at them, didn't you?" we chided. He couldn't argue with that. However, their being around us all the time bothered him.

A tropical downpour stormed in, and the Sucusari began to rise. We decided it was time to make the trip, loaded our heavy 36-foot canoe with what supplies we would need, and shoved off. The entire village stood on the bank, overlooking the river, watching. We waved good-bye as we drifted from view around the first bend. The river was flowing rather swiftly. With our paddles, we guided the cumbersome canoe past low overhanging branches and tree trunks that were constantly in our path.

We drifted noiselessly down the Sucusari, enjoying the many jungle sounds. Several large caiman, sunning themselves along the shores, slithered into the river as we disturbed their slumber. Numerous blue and gold macaws flew gracefully overhead, scolding us as they passed by, their bright plumage flashing in the dazzling sunlight. Monkeys chattered at us from their treetop sanctuaries, bounding effortlessly from limb to limb.

Families of bats, scurrying from their daytime hiding places under low hanging branches, swooshed past our heads as they darted out.

Breathtakingly beautiful orchids hung from the branches of overhanging trees, making it very difficult to pass by without Ruth wanting to stop and pick a few.

As we approached the mouth of the Sucusari, I cranked up the old Johnson outboard motor, and we shot out into the larger Napo and headed downstream. Just below the mouth of the Sucusari, a large island in the middle of the river loomed ahead of us. The swiftly flowing water careened down the deep channels on both sides of the island. "Which side should we take?" I asked Ruth, who usually sat at the bow of the canoe, to watch for hidden surprises.

The island is about 1/2 mile long and 1/4 mile wide. The local Peruvians grow rice, sugarcane, cassava roots, bananas, and a small watermelon that tastes like cucumber, on the island.

"The left side looks the best today. There doesn't seem

to be as many snags sticking out of the water," Ruth shouted back over the noise of the turbulent river and noisy outboard motor. Sometimes, only one channel is open, due to large chunks of trees that slough off into the river from the torrential tropical rains, and hang up on one side or the other, forcing the river to change its course.

The trip down the Napo was the usual hot, tiring trip, dodging sandbars and up-turned trees and snags. We passed an occasional Peruvian, in his little one-man canoe, paddling along the edge trying to catch something for his next meal.

There is a large island in the middle of the Amazon across from the mouth of the Napo. We decided to make it that far and spend the night, then go on to Iquitos the next morning.

As we nosed the canoe to shore, squadrons of hungry mosquitoes attacked us. I have never seen so many mosquitoes. Clouds of them coming at us from every direction, like squadrons of fighter planes. We had planned on cooking rice for our supper, but the ravenous mosquitoes chased us into our mosquito nets without supper.

The next morning, we dumped everything into the canoe as fast as we could and left. Our bodies were covered with welts.

About halfway to Iquitos, a violent storm hit, making traveling difficult, and very wet. We arrived drenched. We checked into the Peru Hotel, and after a hot shower and change of clothes, we headed for our favorite restaurant. We ordered the usual *Plato Atomico* before going to bed on a spring mattress. Pure luxury!

How we wished we could have spent a week or more, but we promised the Indians we would be back in five days, and we wanted to keep that promise. We were enjoying just being alone for a few days.

We packed all our purchases into the canoe: rice, flour, a few special treats, several rough-sawn mahogany boards, and two 15-gallon drums of gasoline and kerosene. We were heavily loaded, but we left a small space for Ruth at the bow, and a place for me at the stern. The rest was covered with a tarp.

We had just passed the sloping green fields of a rather large farm, when we heard the sound of another motor bearing down on us from behind. A larger cabin boat pulled up alongside.

"You look like *Gringos*," the English speaker shouted at us above the drone of the motors. I shut off my motor so I could hear.

"Yes, we are," we told him.

"Where are you going so heavily loaded?"

"We work among the Orejon Indians up the Napo River."

"My name is Jim. I am an American from Florida down here buying tropical fish. I am going up the Napo. Would your wife like to ride along with us and be more comfortable?"

He didn't have to ask twice. Ruth was happy to relinquish her cramped quarters for a chance to walk around while traveling.

The twenty-seventh chapter of the book of Acts tells of the shipwreck as Paul was being taken to Rome to appear before Caesar. Verse 28, "And they took soundings and found it to be 20 fathoms...."

I had never understood how "they took soundings." I learned that from my travels on the rivers of Peru. A heavy weight is tied to the end of a long rope. Knots are tied every meter along the rope. As the boat travels, a man stands at the bow and tosses the weight into the river. By watching the knots, he can tell how deep the river is. Because of the many hidden sandbars, this exercise is done frequently.

Because it was almost 5:00 p.m., I was expecting Jim to find a place to spend the night. However, just before we arrived at the mouth of the Napo, Jim's captain turned on the boat's search lights. We weren't going to stop.

I never did like the mouth of the Napo. When the water in the Amazon is higher than the Napo, a large whirlpool forms. Peruvians told us many have lost their lives as the whirlpool sucked their small canoes into the whirling eye, and then spat them out downriver, drowned.

The pilot of Jim's boat knew of the whirlpool, so he kept to the far side of the river. I was following close behind when my motor ran out of gas. I began frantically dumping gasoline into the tank. Just before I drifted to the churning water, I cranked the engine and it started on the first try. It usually didn't. With full throttle, the canoe began to pull free and I was able to catch up with Jim's boat. I gave a big sigh and a prayer of thanks.

By now it was starting to get pretty dark. There was no moon, so I had to keep as close to Jim's boat as possible. I had no idea how far he was planning to travel before stopping.

We had been traveling for about an hour when the shear pin on my outboard motor broke. As I began floating downstream, I shut off the motor. The little light in front of me slowly faded and soon disappeared. Ruth didn't know I was no longer following.

"Lord, You know where I am. I don't. You know where Ruth and the others are, I don't. If I am to get out of this alive, it is going to have to be Your doings," I prayed.

Fortunately, I had placed my toolbox next to my feet, and I knew where the shear pins were located. As I drifted down the Napo River in total darkness, I managed to get the heavy motor off the transom and onto the tarp. I removed the propeller and replaced the shear pin. I then lifted the motor back onto the transom and tightened the screws that held it in place. All by feeling.

The night was as black as the inside of a tar pot. All I could see was the faint outline of the tree tops on both sides of the river.

By looking at the tree tops, I pointed the canoe upstream and started the motor. My next thoughts were of the many sandbars, the sunken tree trunks, or the small islands floating downstream to meet me. Any of these could spell disaster.

By watching the tree tops, I traveled up the winding river, not knowing where I was going. I had no idea where Ruth was. After traveling for what seemed like hours, I spotted a faint light in the distance and headed for it—and there they were, stopped for the night. Were we ever glad to see each other!

"When we stopped and I didn't hear your motor, I knew something was wrong. All I could do was pray. I didn't know what else I could do. I didn't even know how I would spend the night because you had the mosquito nets and sleeping bags. If you had drowned, I don't know what I would have done," Ruth said.

"The Lord took care of us and brought us through. By noon tomorrow we will be back in our house in the village. All things did work out—a bit scary—but they worked out. Besides, we had a special Someone with us."

"Who?"

"Our personal Angel."

15 | The Big Snake

WE AROSE AT DAYBREAK, THANKED JIM FOR MAKING the trip more enjoyable for Ruth, and headed up the Napo for the Sucusari. We were thankful for the clear weather the entire trip, but we were concerned about the water level of the Sucusari. Several days of no rain could mean the river would be too low for travel. However, as we approached the mouth, we could see there was lots of water shooting out into the Napo. There would be plenty of water to get to the village without having to chop our way through.

Around noon we nosed into the bank just below the village. Everyone was standing on the bank waiting for us and immediately came down to help us unload. We had purchased a kilo of hard candy and handed several pieces to each. A real treat.

We noticed Irisi was not among them. "Where is Irisi?"

"Federico from the Napo came and took her for his wife."

We didn't make any comment, but we could see by the look on Hilario's face that he was terribly hurt. After working for more than a year for Irisi, he was not going to get her after all. We felt sorry for him.

Irisi had been to Iquitos and had seen the contrast between life with her people, and the better life in the big city. She wanted the better life. She probably envisioned marrying a Peruvian would give her that better life. More material things and more freedom. She may have envisioned life to be ice cream and cake, but she was soon to learn it didn't work out that way. In the first place, she didn't speak Spanish. She would be alone among strangers.

For us, life returned to normal. We were busy learning the language and doing what teaching we could to prepare them for their eventual transition into the Spanish culture.

When we first arrived in the village, there was only the one extended family. Eight people in all. Now there were twenty-seven living at the village, all trying to crowd into the one communal house. Food for so many also created a problem. More cassava roots and plantains had to be planted.

One day, as we were sitting on the edge of the big house, Daniel walked by with live coals. They use the slash and burn method of farming. Trees and brush are cut down and left to dry in the sun. Then the dried cuttings are set on fire. Crops are planted in the burned-off area between the charred tree limbs and trunks.

With the live coals, Daniel was about to set fire to the plot of ground that had been cleared near the village.

Smoke had just begun to billow up when Daniel yelled, "*Haianya! Haianya!*"

I hadn't learned that word, but I knew he had spotted something unusual, so I grabbed my .22 rifle and headed for the smoke.

"*Hunibaima! Hunibaima!*" they all called to me. "Don't

kill it! Don't kill it!"

When I got to Daniel, there was so much fire and smoke I couldn't see anything. "What is *haianya*? I asked.

Hai means big, and *anya* means snake—big snake. I didn't know how big, and I couldn't see it, so I walked back to the house.

Later that afternoon the fire and smoke died down, so we went looking for *haianya*. There it was coiled up under a large log—a water boa about 20 feet long and 7 inches in diameter. It didn't move but kept its beady eyes on us.

As I raised my rifle to kill it, they again hollered in very excited voices, "*Hunibaima! Hunibaima! Hunibaima!*"

"Why?" I asked.

"If you kill it, all our babies will die and all our bones will ache."

I didn't worry about their aching bones because we were frequently dispensing aspirins for achy bones, but the thought of a baby dying (and Ruth's insistence), kept me from shooting it. The Tylee's experience in Brazil flashed through my mind.

"If you kill it, and one of their babies should die, we would be blamed," Ruth said. I didn't like the thought of so large a snake living near our house; besides, I wanted the skin. But I took Ruth's advice and didn't shoot it.

Later that evening, I walked to where we had seen the snake, but it was gone. I assumed it had slithered into the river and gone somewhere else.

Tito, the chief's son, was probably our favorite little boy. He seemed to enjoy being around us and we enjoyed his company.

A few days had gone by when Tito came to me and whispered. "I know where *haianya* is."

"Where?" I asked. He then took me by the hand and led me a short distance from the village, to a small clearing. The snake was stretched out full length in the sun. At night, it coiled itself under a log, but the next day, it would again come out to sun itself. The Indians were getting a bit nervous having the snake so close to the village.

The next morning, Miguel walked over to me and announced, "We're going to the chief's house to drink *ayahuasca* to find out why the snake is staying here."

"You're going to leave Ruth and me here by ourselves while you are gone?"

"Yes."

"What if the snake comes down to the house while you are gone? May I kill it?"

The men of the tribe got their heads together and made a decision. "If *haianya* comes to the village while we're gone, you may kill it."

As the people got into their canoes, I asked, "When will you be back?"

"We'll be back in three days, as soon as we find out why *haianya* is staying near the village."

Ayahuasca acts as a mind-expanding drug made from the bark of a certain tree. It produces images in the mind. As an example, if one of their members failed to return from a long trek through the jungle and they wanted to know where he was, they would drink *ayahuasca* and the *ayahuasca* would show them where he was. They now wanted the *ayahuasca* to show them why *haianya* was staying near the village.

Shortly after the Indians left, I cut a long pole and made a slit in the smaller end. I then got a long rope and made a loop in one end. By placing the noose in the slit, I was able to work the rope around the snake's head and pull it down to the village clearing where I shot it in the head. Once I got it uncoiled, it slid along the ground like a log. They hadn't specified how it should get to our clearing, so I made it easy for the snake.

We then heard the distant drone of an outboard motor making its way up the river. Soon Phil, a missionary working among the Peruvians along the Napo River, nosed his canoe into the bank just below our house.

"Hi, Phil. You came just at the right time," I said with somewhat of a smile on my face.

"Why did I come at the right time?" Phil answered.

"I just killed a water boa and need you to help me skin it."

"I'm not sure I'm going to like this," Phil countered with a hint of apprehension in his voice.

Darkness was beginning to settle on us, so we decided to get busy and skin the snake. Ruth held the kerosene lantern, Phil pulled on the tail while I began skinning. Each time I cut, the nerve reaction caused it to coil. Phil would pull on it to straighten it out and I would make another cut. Skinning the snake was harder than we thought. It took us more than two hours to skin it. Then we learned why it was staying near our village.

Anacondas' babies are born live. It was staying near us because we occupied one of the few cleared spots in the jungle where it could sun itself to mature its eggs. In a few days, we would have had thirty-three baby anacondas slithering around our village and a vicious mother protecting them.

It became too dark, and we were too tired to do anything with the carcass, so we left it until the morning. Early the next morning, we dragged the 200-plus pounds of stinking snake down to our canoe and dumped it in. We then cleaned up the mess of broken snake eggs, swept the area with a broom, then chased the dogs and chicken across the area to make it look "natural." We then paddled a good thirty minutes downstream to where we could drag it into the bushes and bury it. Before we got back into the canoe to return to the village, we tried to fix the area so the Indians wouldn't know where we buried it. Then Phil had to leave.

As we rounded the bend back to the village, three of the chief men were standing on the bank.

"You killed *haianya*, didn't you?"

"Yes, I did. Let me show you where I killed it." I then took them to the spot where I shot the snake.

"He was coming down to kill our dogs," one of them commented. I didn't say anything.

"How did you know I killed it?" I wanted to know.

"While drinking *ayahuasca*, we saw you."

"How did I kill it?" I asked.

"You killed it with a stick," they said.

"No, I didn't," I said. "I shot it with my rifle." Later as I thought about it, they were not familiar with .22 rifles. Did the .22 rifle look like a stick to them? They must have seen something, because they were not to return for three days. This was only the morning of the next day.

"Did you skin it?" Miguel asked.

"Yes, I did."

"I thought you did, because I can see where you dragged the carcass to the canoe. You made a real mess," Miguel responded.

"Why don't you put the skin in the sun to dry it so it doesn't spoil?" Miguel suggested. Actually, they all seemed very relieved that the snake was gone. I certainly was.

A few days later, I was traveling downriver with several of the men when we passed the spot where we buried the snake.

"That's where you buried *haianya*," one of the men blurted out as he pointed to the spot. There was no way we could fool them.

While the skin was in the sun drying, Maria wouldn't even go close to it. She wouldn't look at it. When it was thoroughly dry, I put it in a sack and hid it under our bed so Maria, the old grandmother, couldn't see it. She was very superstitious about snakes. To her, snakes represented evil.

16 | Changing Gears

ROMERO WAS ONE OF THE MANY WHO CAME TO LIVE in our tiny village. We soon realized he was very intelligent, and we looked to him as the possible future leader of the tribe. Somewhere, he had learned more Spanish than the rest of his people. If we were to guess his age, we would place him somewhere between seventeen and twenty-two.

Romero took an immediate liking to us and was eager to teach us his language. Miguel was willing to teach us, but he was not as sharp as Romero. Romero could anticipate what we were looking for in the construction of their language and would tell us. Miguel would only repeat the words we asked for.

With Romero, we continued making excellent progress. However, we were constantly being interrupted to take care of all sorts of needs. Because of the crowded conditions, two of the men got into a fight. One of them received a nasty cut on the head by a machete. It was time to get out the medicine kit again.

Ruth kept busy working with the women, teaching them to sew and keeping the sewing machine running. Several became quite adept at sewing on the machines. After the chief's wife, Nieves, learned to sew, we sent one of the machines to her house for her family to use. The other remained on our porch.

We had not seen Herman nor the *Senora* for a long time. Since I began working with Romero, Miguel spent a lot of time hunting and had collected a number of wild pig skins and smoked meat. He wanted a pair of shoes.

"Miguel, why don't we make a trip to Iquitos to sell your hides and smoked meat? And you can buy yourself a pair of shoes."

Miguel's eyes brightened and a big grin spread across his face as he responded with the usual "*Dea.*"

There was plenty of water in the Sucusari as we shoved off and glided down the river. Although Ruth and I had tried to cover our tracks where we buried the snake, Miguel's eyes were too keen. "That's where you buried the snake," he said as he pointed to the shore. He too was right.

The Orejones are jungle people and know where they are at all times. They would sometimes take me along on their hunting trips. Although we couldn't see the sky because of the intertwining branches of the tall tropical trees, they knew where we were. The jungle looked the same to me no matter in which direction I looked, but not to them.

"The big river (Napo) is that direction and our house is that direction," one of them would assure me. Had they not been with me, I wouldn't have had the foggiest idea where I was.

On another one of our trips through the jungle, I started to step over some fallen limbs. "Don't do that, there is a small snake that is very poisonous that can jump and bite you on the neck. They hide under fallen limbs." They taught me a lot about living in the jungle.

No sooner had we entered the Napo River when a tropical downpour hit us. It was raining so hard we couldn't travel, so we headed for the first house we saw.

"May we stay here until the rain quits?" we asked the owner, *Senor* Carmelo. He gave us the usual courtesy answer, "My house is your house." We expected the rain to quit, but it didn't. Miguel stayed at the canoe to keep it bailed out and to make sure the tarp didn't blow off, allowing the cargo to get wet.

We realized the rain wasn't going to quit, so we spent the night there. Some of the meat did get a little wet, so we dried it over *Senor* Carmelo's fire. After an early breakfast of smoked meat and cassava root, we shoved off for Iquitos. The weather was hot and humid for the rest of the trip.

The bustling port in Iquitos was a welcome sight after two days on the Amazon.

As soon as we tied up the canoe, we took the meat and skins to the open air market and sold them for a reasonably good price. I gave all the money to Miguel. He had never had money in his hand before and really didn't know what to do with it.

"Put the money in your pocket and let's go buy you a pair of shoes." With that, we trudged off to one of the shoe stores. Miguel picked out a pair of black leather shoes, his very first pair of shoes. I don't know if they fit or not, but he wanted them. I helped him count out the money.

He looked so proud wearing shoes. We left the store and I wish I could have taken a movie of him walking. He walked as though he were on stilts—stiff-legged. About a block down the street, he took off his shoes and carried them under his arm. Walking without shoes was much more comfortable for him.

"I would like to buy a new pair of pants and a shirt," Miguel said. We went into a store and purchased a new pair of trousers and a colorful new shirt. He was in "hog heaven."

"Do I have money enough to buy a new shotgun?" he asked.

"Yes, you have money for a shotgun." He purchased a new shotgun and a full box of shells. He had never owned a full box of shells in his life. The *Senora* would only give out five shells to each man, and then demand a skin for each shell she gave. He also bought colorful cloth for his wife Maria and his daughter Isidora.

One other thing he wanted. Salt. In the past they had to depend upon the *Senora* for salt. She would give them a kilo of salt for several pig skins. She would then tell them they still owed her for the salt.

Salt was controlled by the government of Peru. We had to go to the salt depository to buy a sack of salt. They were out of salt. "We expect a ship to come in tomorrow bringing salt. Come back tomorrow afternoon," the man in charge told us.

We had planned on leaving that same day, but now we had to wait until the next day to leave.

Eating in restaurants was a new experience for Miguel. He had never been to one before. In the tribe, the only knife they have is their machete.

As I was demonstrating how to use a fork and knife, Miguel said in Spanish *"Hay que aprender."* ("It is necessary to learn.") He did quite well for a beginner.

The next day we were at the salt depository at one in the afternoon, and the salt was there. Miguel purchased a 50-kilo bag and still had 500 *soles* left.

"What do I do with the rest of the money?"

"Miguel, you are going to need money later on. Take it home with you and keep it. It's yours.

Late the next afternoon, when we pulled into the bank below the village, everyone was there to greet us and came down to see what Miguel had bought. He proudly displayed his new shotgun, his new shoes, his new store-bought pants and shirt, and all the other things he had purchased. He didn't put on his new shoes, though, he just tied them to the roof pole above his hammock for everyone to see.

The item that impressed them most was the sack of salt. Never in their entire lives had they had so much salt. Now they could smoke all the wild meat they wanted without asking the *Senora* for salt.

Ruth and I decided it was time to go back to Yarina and take Romero with us. He agreed to go. However, for some reason, he needed to return to his village on another river several days by trail from the Sucusari.

"When will you be back?" we asked Romero.

"I will return in five days."

We called Yarina and asked for a service flight and were told the plane would be in our area in five days. That was perfect timing.

The next few days were dry and hot, no rain. Slowly the Sucusari began to recede.

"If we don't have rain in the next few days, we won't be able to get out to catch the plane," I commented to Ruth.

The fourth day came and went—no rain. The water was far too low for us to make it to the mouth of the Sucusari, but we continued packing everything for storage for the three months we would be gone.

That night a tropical storm hit us. At daybreak we ran to the river. It was overflowing. As we walked back to the house, Romero came walking out of the jungle. Perfect timing again.

The Sucusari River was filled to overflowing, so we made it to the plane in record time.

Romero took to flying like a seasoned flyer. He didn't get airsick like Miguel and Maria, but thoroughly enjoyed seeing the jungle from a new perspective—looking down at the vastness of the verdant sea that stretched as far as the eye could see.

"Big!" he said.

17 | Yarina Cocha

ROMERO ENJOYED LIFE AT YARINA. OUR *GRINGO* CUL-
ture was such a contrast to his jungle life, including our food.
But he got used to it, especially the cookies, pies, and cakes.

The base at Yarina Cocha kept getting bigger and bigger, so Ruth purchased a used bicycle for me. The bicycle
intrigued Romero, and in a very few tries he mastered it.
Whenever we weren't working on the language, he was out
riding my bicycle on the bumpy roads around the base,
splashing through the water-filled mud holes and having a
wonderful time.

Along with teaching me his language, I was teaching
him to read Spanish. In one week he buzzed through
Primers One and Two. By the time we were ready to return
to the Sucusari, Romero was reading Spanish. We knew he
was intelligent, but we didn't realize just how smart he really was until I began teaching him to read Spanish. He even
read from the dictionary when he wasn't out riding my bicycle or working on the language.

Three months passed by all too quickly. We were getting to where we could converse fairly well in Orejon, but we realized we had to return Romero to his people. We also wanted to see how the people in the village were doing. Our primary concern was the *Senora* and Herman. Had they gained another foothold, or were the Orejones truly free?

Once again we said our good-byes, wedged ourselves into the smaller Aeronca, and were soon airborne for possibly our last trip to the tribe. Five years was the specified time we were to remain on the field before furlough, and we had already passed the five-year mark. It was time to prepare for our return to the United States.

While at the base, we talked with our director about someone else taking over, because we did not feel it wise to leave the Indians for an extended period of time.

A young couple, Dan and Virginia Velie, had recently arrived and were anxious to begin working on a language. They accepted the assignment to continue the work among the Orejones. After intensive Spanish study, they would replace us. In the meantime, we returned to the village until Dan and Virginia were able to take over.

After what seemed like forever, we landed at the waterfront port of Iquitos. We weren't planning on being in the village very long, so we didn't purchase a lot of items. Besides, the small plane was too small to carry very much. Eating with the Indians was OK for short periods of time, but we liked a little more variety. We did purchase a small quantity of rice, sugar, and a few other staples—as much as the pilot would allow us to take.

As we were walking down the main street in Iquitos, Romero began reading all the store signs. One particular store was named *Tienda Romero*. Romero stopped, looked at the sign and said, "That's my name!" We were thrilled.

As we reached the Sucusari, the pilot made a couple of circles over the village to let the people know we were back and for them to paddle our canoe to the mouth of the river.

We waited at the mouth for about an hour before Miguel, Daniel, and Hilario poked the nose of my big canoe into the Napo and paddled upriver, the rhythmic sound of their wide paddles slapping the water. To arrive so quickly, they must have paddled like crazy. In minutes the canoe glided to a stop beside the plane's pontoons.

As is their custom, no one said anything for several minutes. Finally, I asked, "How is everyone?"

"*Dea,*" they all said. However, when we arrived at the village, Irisi was sitting in a hammock in the darker part of the big communal house.

"Why is Irisi here? Isn't she living with Federico on the Napo? Why is she crying?" I questioned. I had a feeling something was very wrong.

"Irisi's husband and two babies drowned in the Napo River," Miguel told me.

"How did that happen?" Then Miguel told me the story.

"Gregorio, from upriver, invited everyone to a *minga* (called barn-raising in the early days of America) to cut his sugarcane and make *chancaca* (raw sugar). Their only pay was lots of food and all the *aguardiente* they could drink. By late afternoon the men were pretty well intoxicated. *Aguardiente* is bad," Miguel added.

"When the work was completed and the people started leaving for home, Irisi headed toward her small canoe with her two small children. 'You go home in your canoe, I'm taking the babies with me,' Federico said as he snatched the babies from her and shoved her away. In her limited Spanish

175

Irisi said, '*Boracho!*' (you are drunk). Federico hit her and knocked her down. She sat for a moment before she got up and walked to her canoe. Federico was already a distance from shore heading slightly upstream against the current.

"Darkness was settling over them as they paddled, so Federico didn't see the tree clump floating toward him until it was too late. A large limb caught his tiny canoe and rolled it over, throwing the three of them into the churning waters. Irisi sat in horror as she watched her two children bob up and down as they floated away from her. She tried to paddle to them, but in an instant they disappeared under the murky water. All three drowned."

"What did she do then?" I asked.

"She went on home but realized she couldn't stay there, so gathered what she could carry in her canoe and came here. It was very dark when she arrived. Since then all she does is sit in her hammock and cry."

I walked over to her, put my hand on her shoulder and said, "I'm very sorry." Irisi said nothing, she just kept looking down, sobbing.

As the days passed she began to regain her composure and started doing things around the house. She didn't speak much, but she had never been much of a talker.

Hilario never gave up hope. He continued doing the things every good prospective son-in-law would do. He carried the water for the house, cut the firewood, and helped supply the food—all the time keeping himself visible to Irisi. When he spoke to her, she didn't answer. She wouldn't even look at him.

Gradually she began to take over some of the household chores—doing the cooking and sweeping up. She seldom left the house. When not busy, she lay in her hammock, slowly swaying back and forth. She missed her children and her life on the outside. This was the only time in her short life she felt free, free from the mores of her tribe. Fate didn't allow her to escape after all. We wondered if now she would be content to marry Hilario and remain in the village.

18 | The Drowning of Tito

RUTH AND I KEPT BUSY IN THE VILLAGE, LEARNING all we could about the language, treating the sick and injured, and teaching Spanish. I also began teaching Romero how to operate the small Penta outboard motor. We planned to leave it with him so he could take their produce to Iquitos to sell.

We had no intention of taking the Indians away from the *Senora* and Herman, but they hadn't left us much choice. It would have made life much simpler for all if they had cooperated, but they wouldn't. I guess greed is the same in all cultures.

We were sure Luis would continue to be their chief, but we hoped Romero would be their business agent and teacher. He eventually did become their teacher (see letter from Romero, Appendix).

One day we were sitting on the edge of the big communal house listening to the chatter of several of the women and writing down new words and phrases, chiming into the

179

conversation whenever we could. Suddenly, we heard Nieves hollering as she ran towards us from her house upriver, "*Tito hunihog*! *Tito hunihog!*" (Tito drowned!)

The river was just perfect for swimming. One of the children's favorite swimming holes was below the chief's house. When the river was at its highest, water cascaded over the top of the large tree that bridged the river. Today the water was just right—the big log was perfect for diving.

Tito decided to go for a swim by himself. He did not know an electric eel was resting on the bottom below the log. When he dove into the water, the eel gave off an electric shock that was strong enough to kill Tito. The electric shock must have caused him to gasp for breath and fill his lungs with water, because he didn't surface. Luis jumped into the river and brought him out of the water, but it was too late. They didn't know about CPR.

Tito's sudden death cast a pall like a dark cloud over the village, and the loud cries of the women and children broke the stillness of the jungle. After about an hour of showing his grief, Luis slowly walked back to his own house, gently cradled Tito's lifeless body in his arms and carried it under his house where he dug a shallow grave and, with tears streaming down his face, placed the body of his son. Soon, several of the men came to cut down the trees close to the house. This was to keep *Mainena* from bothering Tito. Then Luis removed their few personal effects and set fire to the house. This was their custom. They could no longer live in a house that brought back so many memories.

To avenge Tito's untimely death, the electric eel had to die. A few days later, the slow-moving current was perfect for poisoning the water to kill everything in it—especially the eel.

A root containing *rotenone* (which is used in industrial sprays) is gathered in large quantities and pounded to a pulp to release the white milk containing the *rotenone*. The *rotenone* stops the gill action of the fish and they die and float to the surface.

As the men pounded the roots, the women constructed a pole fence downriver to catch the fish.

When the fence was completed, the men washed the pounded roots into the water. As the white milk blended with the water and came in contact with the fish, the fish began coming to the surface. We all stood along the shore, with either spears or baskets, to harvest the catch. The fish that escaped us were caught in the fence. Only one problem—no eel.

Tito's death brought a terrible loss to all of us. We had come to love him very much.

Life again settled down to the usual routine of learning new words and dispensing aspirins for sore joints (probably arthritis), handing out worm pills, and treating the usual wounds.

19 Matriarchal Maria & Other Personalities

GRANDMOTHER MARIA WAS AN INTERESTING PERSON. How old she was we had no idea. We just knew she was too old to hunt anymore. Her skin, from years of exposure to the sun, was as rough as the skin of the caiman that inhabit the rivers, and made her look much older than she may have been. If we were to guess her age, we would put her around seventy.

Because she was no longer able to trek through the jungle, she spent her days taking care of her one chicken and her many jungle friends: several parakeets, a toucan, a baby sloth that ate only leaves from a certain tree, and her *agouti*. Any orphaned or injured bird or animal became a part of her extended "family."

Maria wanted baby chicks, but her hen would only lay eggs; it would not set. Finally, in desperation, she placed ten eggs on an old rag, placed the hen on the eggs, and put a woven basket over the nest. In trying to get out, the hen broke all the eggs. Maria was furious. She scolded the hen and placed ten more eggs under her. The same thing happened.

"Maria, would you like to trade your hen for one we have that lays twelve eggs and sets?"

"I will trade," she replied.

We were both happy. We had a hen that laid an egg every day, and she had Blondie I, the hen that was born to set.

Another problem occurred to further infuriate Maria. Her toucan loved eggs. When Maria wasn't watching, the toucan would stick its long beak under the hen, extract an egg, and fly away with it. To break the egg, as it flew away it would drop the egg, then fly down to consume it. Scolding the toucan didn't help a bit; it just cocked its head and looked at her. But it did relieve Maria's frustration. She never did get any baby chicks.

Her parakeets kept our dog Chichi busy. They had learned to imitate my whistle and kept Chichi running from place to place looking for me. It was like a game they were playing as they flew from limb to limb, imitating my whistle. Chichi never did catch on that it was the parakeets whistling. She just kept running from place to place until she finally spotted me.

Maria considered her animals like family. We caused quite an uproar when we butchered our first chicken.

"Why did you kill the chicken?" she wanted to know in a rather accusative voice.

"We wanted to eat it," was our reply.

"If you had children, you wouldn't eat them, would you?"

"No."

"Then why did you kill your chicken?"

From then on, we could only kill a chicken when Maria wasn't around.

Maria's grandson was the problem child of the village. Of the several children now living in the village, Mateo was the "*picaro*." He loved to use his machete, and for a boy of around ten, he was very good with it—too good.

We had planted an avocado tree near the communal house. The tree was growing nicely and was just beginning to bear fruit. In a week or two, we would have had avocados, except for Mateo and his machete. One day, he cut down the tree as Maria and his parents, Daniel and Isidora, looked on, not saying a word. They thought it was funny. We didn't.

His next target was a papaya tree. It suffered the same fate. The Orejones only eat what grows or lives in the jungle, except for the bananas and cassava roots they plant near the village; therefore, the avocado and papaya trees were not important.

The Orejones never punished their children, no matter what they did. They would, however, ask Ruth to punish them—which she never did. She would, however, make a game of punishing them, hoping the message would get across that we didn't approve of their being "naughty." I don't think it worked.

Mateo was a typical young boy full of energy. He had to be busy doing something, and cutting down trees was his thing, but we loved him.

Life for Mateo was exciting. Another of his many activities was swimming. A low branch, that poked its arm over the river just below the village, served as the diving board. When the river was high enough, he and the other children spent hours jumping into the river.

Another sport was shooting small birds with his blowgun. The tips of the darts were dipped in a black tar-like poison made from the juices of certain roots. Once hit, the bird dies within four minutes. The poison attacks the nerve centers of the bird or animal. He brought home lots of little birds.

We really did enjoy Mateo in spite of all his antics. He was just a typical boy with bounding energy. His long, jet-black hair was usually tousled. His white teeth were set like gems in his sun-darkened face. His dark brown eyes danced with excitement, and his round face seemed permanently frozen in a smile.

One day, Mateo came to me with a chunk of the soft pulp from the inside of a pona palm tree. "Will you carve me an elephant?" he asked. He had seen pictures of elephants in the magazines we had brought along.

The pulp was very soft and spongy and hard to carve, but I made what looked something like an elephant. At least it had a long trunk, and Mateo really enjoyed that funny-looking elephant. The only toys they had were rubber balls made from jungle rubber (a bit more round than square), and a spin top made from a jungle nut.

Mateo had a keen mind. Each time I taught his father and others the Spanish numbering system, Mateo was there learning.

————

Concentrated hunting was the villagers' antidote against the boredom of life. When life became too humdrum, they either whipped up a batch of fermented cassava root and had a good bash, or they went on extended hunting trips at the headwaters of the Sucusari.

More than once I patched their severe machete cuts after a drunken brawl. Fortunately, their drunken brawls didn't happen very often. When they did, they lasted until all the fermented *masato* was gone.

Their extended hunting trips provided an opportunity to earn money. And now that they were free to do their own trading, they were able to purchase more things they needed and wanted.

It was on one of these extended hunting expeditions, when Ruth and I were sleeping in the same hut with Miguel and Maria, that I got a glimpse into their beliefs and legends. I was almost asleep when Miguel whispered, "Roberto."

"What, Miguel?" I asked.

"Do you hear that noise?" The only noises I could hear were the usual nightly jungle noises, especially the shrill monotonous high-pitched mating call of the cicadas.

"What do you hear, Miguel?" I asked.

"Don't you hear *Mainena*? He is in the tree tops."

I still didn't hear anything unusual, so I went back to sleep. Our task was again defined—to give the Orejones the Bible in their own language as soon as possible.

"Do you know where the monkeys came from?" Daniel asked one day, as we were sitting in the house. A heavy tropical downpour was pelting the roof and cascading off the eves. It was too wet to be outside. The tropical downpour must have reminded Daniel of the story.

"Where did the monkey come from?" I answered. I knew this story was going to be interesting.

"One day, long ago, our people were sitting in their house. It was raining just like it is now. It had been raining for several days, and they were running out of food. One of the men looked up into the tree tops and spotted some fruit.

"'I am going to go to the tree top and get that fruit,' he said. 'But how am I going to get there?'

187

"'I know,' he said. 'I will tie a vine around my waist, climb to the top, and fasten myself up there with the vine while I collect the fruit.'

"With that, he climbed to the top of the tree and liked it so much he has been there ever since," Daniel concluded.

Nancy was the shy little daughter of the chief. She never said much, but, like Mateo, she smiled a lot and was always close at hand. Her round face was framed by her dark hair and highlighted by her beautiful playful eyes.

We were all sitting on our porch when I picked up Nancy and put her on my lap. She was about four years old.

"I'm going to take you home with me," I teased. Her parents didn't realize I was teasing. Another mistake of doing what we often do in our culture—tease. They don't. Well, they don't, usually.

"Take her!" both parents said in unison.

I had a hard time explaining my way out of that one.

They do have a sense of humor, though. One day Daniel brought in a wild pig. It didn't have a mark on it—no blood visible anywhere.

"How did you kill the pig?" I asked.

"I grabbed him by the tail and killed him with my hands," he said without smiling. The wild pigs don't have tails big enough to grab. Finally, he looked at me with a big grin on his face. He never did tell me how he killed it. I figured he saw it swimming in the river and drowned it by holding its head under water.

Luis considered himself as the chief, although we couldn't see where he had much influence in the tribe. He did have the largest discs in his ear lobes, though. Before the white man came, the ear discs were a symbol of rank in the tribe. However that didn't seem to be the case anymore.

Luis did carry himself with a certain air of superiority. His long, straight hair, slightly tinged with streaks of gray, hung loosely down his back, his bangs trimmed neatly just above his eyebrows. More than the others, he kept his face streaked with black and red markings. The others only painted their faces occasionally.

Thinking corn would be a good supplement to their diet, we shared enough corn for them to plant a small garden— corn we had purchased for our own use.

Near the village they had cleared an area for planting plantains and cassava roots. Among the cassava roots and plantains, Luis began jabbing a pointed stick into the ground to make a hole. He then placed four corn kernels in the hole.

Knowing he would soon run out of kernels, I suggested, "In our country we only put two kernels in each hole."

As he jabbed the stick into the ground, he said in a very authoritative way, "In my country we put four," as he dropped in four kernels.

The corn grew tall and the ears full. When it was time to harvest the corn, we assumed they would hang the ears above the fire table to harden the corn for later use. We assumed wrong.

When all the corn was harvested, they placed the kernels in a large earthenware pot and made a very potent alcoholic drink. Then they had a big party. Before giving them the corn, we hadn't thought it through as to what they would do with the harvested corn. Ruth made cornbread; they made liquor. We concluded that giving them corn was not a good idea.

20 | Welcome Dan and Virginia

FINALLY THE DAY CAME. "SUCUSARI, THIS IS YARINA, over," the voice on the other end of the radio waves said. There was no way two people could talk at the same time by radio, so we always said, "over" to let the other party know we wanted them to continue.

"This is Sucusari, over."

"A flight will be coming your way tomorrow to bring Dan out to be introduced to the tribe. Will you be able to meet him at the plane? Over."

"Yes, there is plenty of water in the river now. We will be there." We had already explained to the people that we were returning to our country and Dan and Virginia would be living in our house to learn their language.

"*Dea*," they all said.

The next morning, we heard the drone of the plane's engine as it circled overhead to let us know it had arrived. Three of us jumped into my big canoe and headed downriver.

The entire village stood on the bank of the Sucusari when we returned with Dan. We walked up the bank and all followed, silently, to our house. Finally, I introduced Dan to the people.

"Ruth and I have to return to our country. Dan, and his wife Virginia, will be living in our house and will be learning your language. Virginia will be coming out soon."

How does one say good-bye to a people one has come to love, knowing your good-byes will probably be forever? It's hard.

To avoid showing partiality in disposing of things we no longer needed, we invited all the people to our house. Everything was placed in a big heap on the floor, and at the signal, everybody went for their "treasure." The floor was bare in a flash. Everyone had something, held tightly cradled in their arms.

Ruth and I gathered up the few items we were taking with us and slowly walked down the slippery bank to our canoe. My 36-foot canoe took us down the familiar Sucusari for the last time. The river was full of water, so it didn't take us very long to get to the waiting plane that would return us to Yarina Cocha.

It was now up to Dan and Virginia to complete the work we had started.

Appendix

Señor   Robertos   Sandberg.

Mi muy estimado hermano en Cristo no sabiendo como saludarle de
su auesncia dé mucho tienpo me pongo a escribir para poder saludarle con miles de saludos con todos la familias de Ud.
  Despues de saludarle a Ud. con cariñosamente quiero conuni-
carle unas cuantas palabras.
  Primero quiero agradeser a Ud. con muchicima gracias, que
Dios le bendigue por el gasto que has echo por mí para conprar
la maquina de escribir. Ya he recibido la maquina de escribir
de parte del Sr. Dan Velie.   Nada mas que decirte a Ud. yo ciempre
sigo trajando en la Escuela Bilingüe Mixta # 1971 de Pto. Huamán en
Yanayacu en río Napo. Siempre haste orar por nosotros .

Se despide su amigo que nuca le lolvida, que Dios guarde a Ud.

                              Romero Ríos Ochoa.

                              Romero Ríos Ochoa

                              Iquitos, 8 de Set., 1971

Dear Bob and Ruth;

     Greeting from Peru,. I'll just add a bit to Romero's note.
He just made a trip in here to Iquitos and left about four o'clock
this morning. He came across the Mazán crossover. I asked if he
had written to you yet and he hadn't so he wrote this note to send.
On July the 12th when he was last in, we were able to get him a nice
Spanish made typwriter from Casa Garcia, Marca: Florida de Luxe.
It was one that had been bought in before the importation tax was
imposed here so he had a bit of cash left over which he spent toward
fixing his 10-12. He was very happy to have the typewriter. He
thought maybe you could get him one up there on time and he could
pay you back a little at a time. He understands a now that it was
a gift and appreciates it. He never could have gotten one very
easily here on his own as he has alot of expenses with five kids
now. I just helped him get all his documents strightened out so
we a are sending them in inorder that he might get the allowance
for familia numerosa which will be a big help for him. I was glad
to be able to spend some more time with him just now as he was
rather discouraged. As you know how the people get jealous and
acuse him of making money off their children and that they aren't
learning, etc.etc.. There is still lots of drinking and witheraft
on that river too, so he really needs our prayers. The priests have
been up to his place several times and given him religious materials
for the school and so it goes. Thanks you for your prayers for him
and the work here in general. Josías and I are translating I John
3 this week. We just finished recording on cassette another hour
and 1/2 of scriptures but we haven't had copies made yet needed
for distribution. Bryan just got back yesterday from the Ampiyacu
river and said that our people had taken good care of the player and
appreciated recieving a new cassette. We are encouraged for that.
                                   In Jesus our Lord,
                                   Dan & Virginia

On September 1971, I received the above letter from Dan and Romero. We were thrilled to learn the Indians are truly free and that Romero had completed the Teacher Training Course at Yarina and was now the tribal teacher.

It was also wonderful to know he was learning to use the typewriter Ruth and I had sent money for, and to realize how far he had come from when we first had met him.

A few years ago he was just another jungle boy living much as his ancestors had lived for hundreds of years. Because of the backing of the Peruvian government, the Orejones have entered into the twentieth century.

When the chief, Luis, died, we were told he was singing Christian hymns Dan and Virginia had translated into their language. These things have made all the difficulties we encountered in gaining their freedom worthwhile.

Glossary

Agouti	A tropical burrowing rodent about the size of a Chihuahua
Aguardiente	Sugarcane whiskey
Albarengas	Large canoes, split length-wise and made into larger boats by adding hand-hewed boards. These modified canoes are capable of hauling large amounts of cargo.
Caiman	South American alligator
Cushmas	A muu-muu like garment made from hand-spun, hand-woven wild cotton, sewn up both sides but leaving spaces for arms and head
Dea	Good, very good
Don	Means Sir in Spanish
Freeboard	The distance from the water to the top edge of the sideboard

Gringo	A foreigner, especially when of English or American origin
Mainena	Their tribal god. The large ear discs the men wear replicate their god who lives on the moon. We were in the village when there was an eclipse of the moon. As the sun slowly moved to "eat" the moon, the entire tribe began pounding on the trees, shouting, and doing anything they could to make noise to keep the sun from eating their god. Naturally, it worked, because *Mainena* was not eaten by the sun. I then took a ball we had given them, and a flashlight, and tried to show them what actually happened when there is an eclipse. I'm not sure my explanation made any sense to them, but I tried.
Masato	Drink made from fermented cassava root
Nanay River	A very winding, slow-moving river that flows southeast and empties into the Amazon just below Iquitos
Patron	(accent on the 'o') A person designated by the government to protect the Indians, but in all the cases I saw, they exploited the Indians.
Peccary	Wild pig
Picaro	A mischievous person
Pijuayo	(Pihuayo) A jungle fruit shaped somewhat like a Roma tomato. Though hard when green, it softens when ripe and has the texture of cooked potato.

Rosewood	A tree from which is extracted an oil used in the manufacture of perfumes
Sajino	(Sahino) Another type of wild pig
Senor	Mr. — pronounced Senyor
Senora	Mrs. — pronounced Senyora
Shambira	A fiber from the frond of a certain palm tree
Shushupi	A very poisonous pit viper about 12 feet long when fully grown
Tambito	A temporary shelter made from bamboo-like cane, covered with palm fronds.
Tamshi	Long, strong vines hanging from trees in the jungle. The straight grain allows them to be divided and divided and divided until they are as small as a string, which can be woven into thick, strong ropes.